THE ADOBE PHOTOSHOP
elements
CRAFTS BOOK

Elizabeth Bulger

Peachpit
Press

THE ADOBE PHOTOSHOP ELEMENTS CRAFTS BOOK

Elizabeth Bulger

Peachpit

1249 Eighth Street, Berkeley, CA 94710

510/524-2178 (tel) 800/283-9444 (toll-free) 510/524-2221 (fax)

Find us on the World Wide Web at: www.peachpit.com

To report errors, please send a note to errata@peachpit.com

Peachpit is a division of Pearson Education

Copyright © 2006 by Elizabeth Bulger

Editors: Karyn Johnson and Karen Reichstein

Developmental Editor: Cathy Fishel

Production Editor: Pat Christenson

Compositors: Elizabeth Bulger and Stephen Sakowich

Proofreader: Elena Marcus

Indexer: Rebecca Plunkett

Cover design: Aren Howell

Interior and cover photos: Elizabeth Bulger and Stephen Sakowich

Interior design: Elizabeth Bulger and Stephen Sakowich

ISBN 0-321-36896-7

9 8 7 6 5 4 3 2 1

Printed and bound in the United States of America

www.photoshopcrafts.com

To my Mom and Dad, Ethel and Len.

You are the best parents a girl could ever have.

I love you.

ACKNOWLEDGMENTS

My heartfelt thanks go out to so many people who helped make this book possible. To Michael Nolan, who introduced me to the great folks at Peachpit Press: Thank you, Michael. To my Peachpit team—Marjorie Baer, Karen Reichstein, Karyn Johnson, Pat Christenson, Scott Cowlin, Zigi Lowenberg, and Sara Todd—for their amazing amount of support and enthusiasm. To Cathy Fishel, for dotting my I's and crossing my T's, untangling my sentences, and keeping me on track. To David Plotkin, for testing my projects at the last minute, with the greatest attention to detail. To my friends and family, who offered so much encouragement and allowed me to use so many of their great photos. To my husband, Stephen Sakowich, who designed this book with me, and helped get it out the door. It would have been impossible without you. You are my hero, and I love you forever.

CONTENTS

Introduction

CONTENTS

CONTENTS

INTRODUCTION

You've got a digital camera, and now you have a million photos on your computer named IMG0031, IMG0089, IMG0017. . . don't let them languish there: That's a fate worse than a shoebox! Discover your inner-crafter, and share your photos with family and friends in totally new and creative ways using Adobe Photoshop Elements 4 for Windows.

Many of the techniques you learn throughout these pages can be transferred from one project to the next. For example, you can take the techniques used in the Coasters project and use them in the Folding Postcard project to create a special card or invitation. How about changing the Pet Place Mat project into a place mat for your toddler, designed with ABC's, numbers, and other photos? So many possibilities!

Many of the images I use in this book are available on my companion Web site, so if you'd like to follow along using the same images on some of the projects, you can download them by visiting www.photoshopcrafts.com. Since this is a project-oriented book, not every single feature of the program is covered. This is a crafts book, not a manual. However, my publisher, Peachpit Press, offers several outstanding books on Photoshop Elements, as general or as specific in topic as you like. Visit www.peachpit.com to learn more about other Peachpit titles.

This book focuses almost solely on working in the Standard Edit mode. Very few features were added between version 3.0 and 4.0 in that area of the program. So, for those of you who are still working in Version 3.0, I've provided additional information on how to proceed with a particular step in a project that utilizes a new 4.0 tool or command.

I hope this book will inspire you to create a few gifts or keepsakes, while providing some fun learning how to use Photoshop Elements. So, go make some really neat stuff and share it with us on the www.photoshopcrafts.com Web site.

PHOTOSHOP ELEMENTS BASICS

If you've never used Photoshop Elements before, this chapter is a good place to start. Without overwhelming you with too much detail, it will give you a quick overview of the general work area including the toolbox, menus, and palettes. You'll learn about the Quick Fix mode, how to acquire and organize your images with the Photo Browser and Organizer, some facts on file types and resolution, and how to save your images.

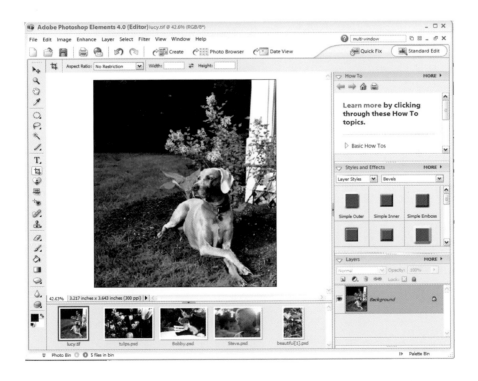

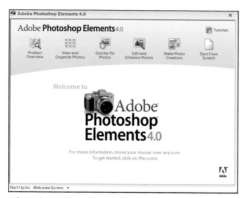

The Photoshop Elements Welcome Screen.

Choose how you want Elements to launch.

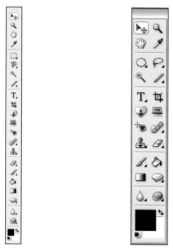

The Toolbox docked.   The Toolbox undocked.

THE WELCOME SCREEN

When you first launch Photoshop Elements, the Welcome Screen appears. It's useful for the first few times you use Elements, while you are familiarizing yourself with the product. It gives a product overview, as well as a place to start for creating projects from scratch, launching tutorials, a way to open images to edit and enhance, and to open the Organizer along with the Photo Browser. Once familiar with Elements, you probably won't want or need the Welcome Screen. In the lower left corner of the screen there is a pop-up menu which lets you choose the way Elements will start up. Here you can choose the Editor or the Organizer. Keep in mind, you can open the Welcome Screen at any time by choosing Window > Welcome while in either the Editor or the Organizer. Since you will be working primarily in the Editor throughout the projects in this book, choose Editor: That's where you'll do most of your Elements magic. The Organizer, on the other hand, is where you go to organize your "database" of images.

THE TOOLBOX

The toolbox offers a variety of tools that you can use for selecting, cropping, painting, retouching, editing, and viewing your images. The toolbox is docked to the left side of the work area and displays a single column of tools. You can undock it by clicking and dragging the top of it away from the edge. It will then display in the more familiar two-column format found in most other Adobe products.

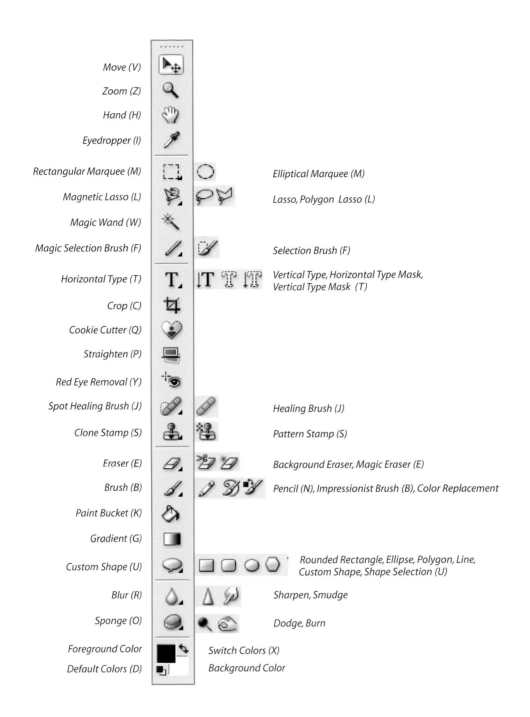

Move (V)

Zoom (Z)

Hand (H)

Eyedropper (I)

Rectangular Marquee (M)   Elliptical Marquee (M)

Magnetic Lasso (L)   Lasso, Polygon Lasso (L)

Magic Wand (W)

Magic Selection Brush (F)   Selection Brush (F)

Horizontal Type (T)   Vertical Type, Horizontal Type Mask, Vertical Type Mask (T)

Crop (C)

Cookie Cutter (Q)

Straighten (P)

Red Eye Removal (Y)

Spot Healing Brush (J)   Healing Brush (J)

Clone Stamp (S)   Pattern Stamp (S)

Eraser (E)   Background Eraser, Magic Eraser (E)

Brush (B)   Pencil (N), Impressionist Brush (B), Color Replacement

Paint Bucket (K)

Gradient (G)

Custom Shape (U)   Rounded Rectangle, Ellipse, Polygon, Line, Custom Shape, Shape Selection (U)

Blur (R)   Sharpen, Smudge

Sponge (O)   Dodge, Burn

Foreground Color   Switch Colors (X)

Default Colors (D)   Background Color

A Tool Tip identifies a tool.

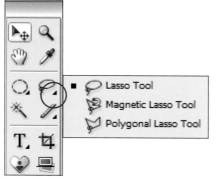

A small black triangle indicates there are hidden related tools in the extended menu.

IDENTIFYING A TOOL IN THE TOOLBOX

To identify a tool, float your mouse pointer over a tool in the toolbox and pause without clicking. A tool tip appears displaying the name of the tool as well as the shortcut key. If you click on the name, which is a link, the Adobe Help Center opens with information about the tool. The previous page identifies all of the tools in the toolbox.

SELECTING A TOOL IN THE TOOLBOX

A black triangle on a tool button indicates that there are related tools in an extended menu. To access the hidden tools, click and hold on the main tool until the extended menu appears.

USING SHORTCUT KEYS TO SELECT A TOOL

Each tool has a one-letter shortcut key (see previous page). You will absolutely speed up your workflow if you take the time to learn these one-letter shortcuts, as there is no need to travel away from your image, and over to the toolbox. Switching between tools is instantaneous. For example, pressing L a few times will toggle you through the three Lasso tools; Pressing C will activate the Crop tool; Pressing V will activate the Move tool.

The Options bar displays specific settings for each tool in the toolbox.

ABOUT THE OPTIONS BAR

The information in the Options bar, located at the top of your work area, changes dynamically every time you select a different tool in the toolbox. It displays relevant settings and options for each tool. For example, you can change the size of a brush, its opacity and hardness setting, and the style as well, all within the Options bar. In addition, when you select a tool, all related hidden tools in the toolbox are also displayed in the Options bar and can also be selected for use. Take a few minutes to click through the tools in the toolbox (try using the shortcut keys, too), and see how the options for each tool change.

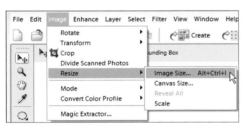

Each pull-down menu is organized by common functions and commands.

THE MENUS

Organized by task, the pull-down menus, located at the top of your work area, offer commands you use while working with your Elements documents. For example, if you want to view your image on screen at a different magnification, you go to the View menu, where you will find different default magnification settings.

Throughout the projects in this book, when you read instructions such as Choose Image > Resize > Image Size, it instructs to first go to the File pull-down menu.

Three default palettes in the Palette Bin.

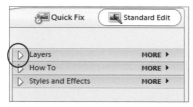

Click the triangle to collapse or open the palettes located in the Palette Bin.

Customize your work area by dragging the palettes you use most often out of the Palette Bin.

THE PALETTES

Elements offers eight palettes that can be opened in the Palette Bin, located on the right side of your work area. By default, the Palette Bin contains the How To, Styles and Effects, and Layers palettes. The other five palettes which are covered throughout the book, can be opened and closed from the Window menu. Here are a few tips for working with palettes:

• Collapse the palettes and open them when you need to by clicking on the white triangle at the top of each palette.

• Drag palettes out of the Palette Bin by clicking on the top bar of the palette and dragging it to the left.

• Reset all palettes to the default settings by choosing Reset Palette Locations from the Window menu.

The Photo Bin holds a thumbnail of
every open image in your work area.

Shuffle through open images.
Show/Hide the Photo Bin.

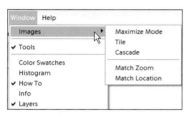

Select a viewing mode for open
documents.

Cascade mode

Tile mode

THE PHOTO BIN

The Photo Bin is located at the bottom of
your work area and displays thumbnails of
all of your open images. Click on one of the
thumbnails to bring it forward to make it
your active document. You can quickly shuffle
through all of the open images by clicking
on the left and right arrows located at the
bottom of the Bin. Click the Show/Hide icon
on the left side of the Photo Bin to toggle its
visibility.

VIEWING MODES FOR IMAGE WINDOWS

There are three basic viewing modes:
Maximize, Tile, and Cascade.

When you have multiple images open, it
can be handy to switch between the different
viewing modes depending on the task at
hand.

You will always want to be in either Cascade
or Tile mode when dragging and dropping
multiple images from one document to
another. If you are working with only one
image, use the Maximize mode. If you are
working with two images, you can rcsize the
image windows using the options in the View
menu, so that you can view both on screen,
and position them side-by-side.

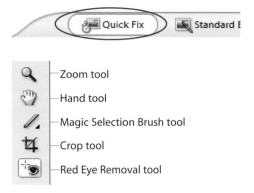

Zoom tool

Hand tool

Magic Selection Brush tool

Crop tool

Red Eye Removal tool

Scribble over the area you want to select with the Magic Selection Brush tool.

A quick Hue adjustment.

QUICK FIX MODE

The Quick Fix mode is handy when you want to apply a few quick edits to an image. When you click on the Quick Fix mode button, you have the options of selecting particular areas of your image for making color adjustments, cropping, and reducing red eye. The Before and After previews show your adjustments instantly. Open the Quick Fix dialog box by clicking the button located at the top-right of your work area. When finished with your quick fixes, click the Standard Edit button to apply the changes to your image.

QUICK FIX WITH THE MAGIC SELECTION BRUSH TOOL

Select the Magic Selection Brush tool and scribble or click over the area you want selected on the After preview image.

If after your first click or scribble, the Magic Selection Brush tool didn't select everything you intended, you can add to the selection by choosing the Indicate Foreground tool (the Magic Selection Brush tool with the "+"), located at the top of the Quick Fix dialog box. Click on the area you want included. If too much of an area is selected, choose the Indicate Background tool, and click on the area you don't want included.

Adjust lighting and color using the palettes on the right side of the Quick Fix dialog box.

Adjust the crop area on the After preview image.

The final crop.

Use the Crop tool to trim your image to the size you wish. Click and drag a marquee over the area on the After preview image and adjust the bounding box by dragging the handles. If you have an exact size in mind, you can enter the dimensions in the Height and Width fields located at the top of the Quick Fix dialog box, and then drag the marquee. Click the check mark to apply the crop. You can also start over, either by pressing the Cancel button, or pressing the Escape (ESC) key on your keyboard. Remember to click the Standard Edit button to exit the Quick Fix dialog box.

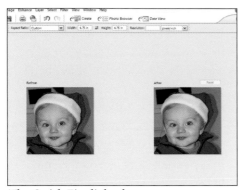

The Quick Fix dialog box.

Before red eye removal.

After red eye removal.

There are several places within Elements where you can choose and apply the Red Eye Removal tool. You can select the tool from the toolbox, select it in Quick Fix mode, or have Elements automatically apply red eye removal while importing images into the Organizer.

In this example, the image is opened in Quick Fix mode. Select the Red Eye Removal tool, and note that, at the top of the work area, you have two settings you can adjust: the size of the pupil and darkness of the pupil. The tool automatically finds the red area within the eye and makes the adjustment for you when you click on the red area. If necessary, make adjustments to the Size and Darkness settings of the pupil area at the top of the work area if the sizing and color are incorrect.

Open the Photo Browser by clicking on this button located at the top of your work area.

You can acquire photos from many different sources.

The Organizer window.

Organize your images by your own criteria.

ACQUIRING AND ORGANIZING PHOTOS

To open your digital images in Photoshop Elements, you need to attach your digital camera, card reader, or mobile phone to your computer. Once attached, the Adobe Photo Downloader searches for the photos and downloads them. If it doesn't, you can still manually download your photos by clicking on the Photo Browser button located at the top of the work area.

When you click on the Photo Browser button, the Organizer opens. Choose File > Get Photos, and then choose your source from the list: camera, card reader, scanner, and so on.

Once your images are in the Organizer, you can sort them by date, organize them based on your own criteria, even tag the faces of family and friends for easy sorting. Working with the Organizer is beyond the scope of this book, however, you may refer to your Elements manual, or online Help file, for more information.

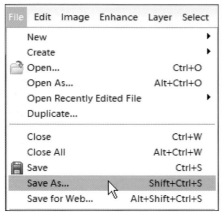

Save a copy of your file by choosing Save As from the File menu.

It's always a good idea to work with a copy of your original image, so you can keep your original intact in case you need it unaltered at a later date. It is strongly recommended that you make a habit of choosing File > Save As, naming the file, and then choosing the .psd (Photoshop Document) file format. That way you know at a glance that your .psd files are working files and not the originals. And, of course, it's a good practice to periodically save while you are working on your image. Choose File > Save and select an appropriate place on your hard drive.

FILE FORMATS

Here is a list of the most common file formats and when to use them:

PSD (Photoshop Document). Use when working in Elements and when you want to keep your layers intact.

JPEG (Joint Photographic Experts Group). Use when sending photos by email or for use on the Web.

GIF (Graphic Interchange Format). For use on the Web for simple animations, images with transparency, and images that include vector graphics and typography, such as logos.

TIFF (Tagged Image File Format). For use with other applications such as page layout, word processing, and graphics programs.

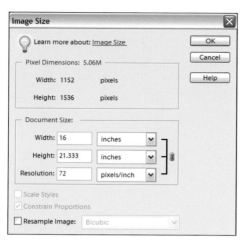

Before adjusting the resolution without resampling the image. It's a big image at a low quality resolution.

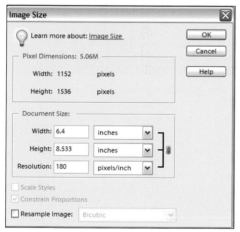

After increasing the resolution, the physical image dimensions are more manageable and the quality will be fine for an inkjet printer.

A NOTE ON RESOLUTION

Every digital image is made up of tiny pixels, or picture elements. Pixels are little squares of color that you can't see unless you've magnified the image.

When you're working with images from a digital camera, the default image resolution is usually 72 ppi (pixels per inch), which gives you an enormous file in terms of its physical dimensions, but a low resolution. 72 ppi is the correct resolution for viewing images on screen, so keep that in mind when you are preparing images for the Web, a slide show, or when sending email. It is, however, too low for a good quality print from an inkjet printer. I recommend resetting the resolution for your camera to at least 180 ppi - 220 ppi. This will give you a quality setting high enough for good results on an inkjet printer, and the physical dimensions of the image will be much more manageable. Your resolution setting needs to be at 300 ppi if your work will be professionally printed.

It's also possible to change the resolution of an image while adjusting the size by Choosing Image > Resize Image Size. For best quality, uncheck Resample Image. In doing so, you can increase the resolution of the image, but the dimensions of the image decrease, and there is no degradation in quality, as you are preserving the total pixel count. Since this topic is beyond the scope of this book, it's suggested you see your product documentation for more information.

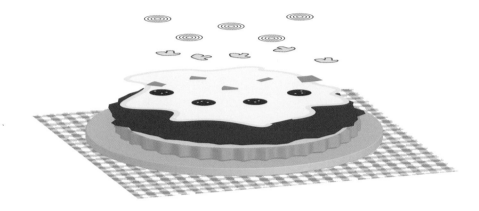

If you plan to do more with your photos than Quick Fix adjustments, touch-ups, and cropping, you will want to gain a solid understanding of how layers work. You use layers when you want to include more than one image and/or other graphic elements in your document. Once you master the use of Photoshop Elements layers, you will wonder how you ever enjoyed life without them. If you want to use this pizza image to learn how to work with layers, you can download it from the www.photoshopcrafts.com Web site.

Compare what you see in the document window to the corresponding layer order in the Layers palette shown here above and below.

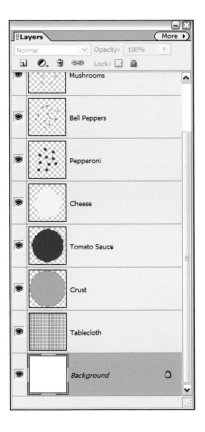

THE LAYERS PALETTE

The Layers Palette enables you to keep track of the different elements that compose your artwork. These elements might include photographs, text, graphics, or painted artwork. Because the Layers palette keeps the different elements independent of one another, you have the freedom and flexibility to experiment, alter, edit, or delete each different item without affecting others. This is called "non-destructive editing."

When you create a new document, download a photo from your digital camera, or scan artwork, and then open the image in Photoshop Elements, the Layers palette displays a thumbnail named "Background". When you add additional layers, either by creating new blank layers or dragging other images into your document, the corresponding layers are named Layer 1, Layer 2, and so on, unless previously named. These additional layers, by default, are always stacked on top of the Background. The stacking order of layers determines how the image is displayed and printed.

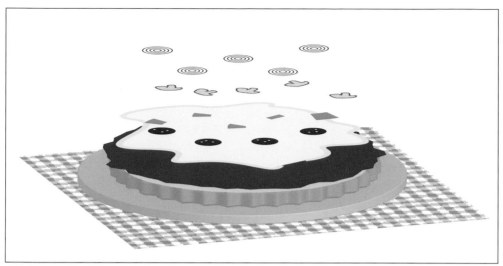

Here's a 3-dimensional view of the stacking order of the layers.

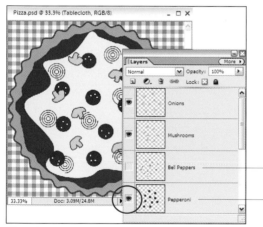

If you're not sure you want peppers on your pizza, temporarily hide that layer by clicking on the Eye icon.

VIEWING AND HIDING LAYERS

When the Eye icon 👁 is displayed in the column to the left of a layer, it indicates that the layer is visible. To temporarily hide a layer, click the Eye icon. You can quickly hide or view multiple layers by dragging up or down the Eye column.

Hidden Layer

Visible Layer

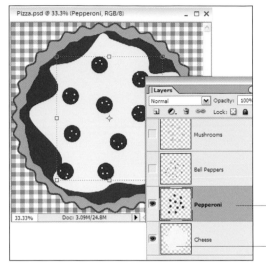

To edit your artwork, you must either select the corresponding layer in the Layers palette, or click on the art in the document window using the Move tool ⯈⊹. The selected layer is also referred to as the active layer.

— Active Layer

— Thumbnail

Click on either the thumbnail or the name of the layer to make it the active layer.

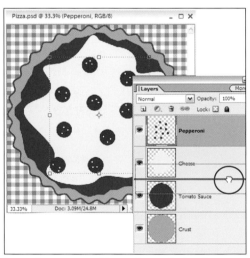

Drag the pepperoni layer beneath the cheese layer.

CHANGING THE STACKING ORDER OF LAYERS

To rearrange the stacking order of the layers, select the layer you want to move and drag it above or below another layer. Release your mouse button when a black line appears between the two layers.

ABOUT THE BACKGROUND

Every image or photo you open in Elements has a Background. You can't move the Background above a layer or put a layer beneath it until you name it. Double+click on the Background thumbnail, enter a new name, and click OK. Elements now considers the Background an actual layer, which will enable you to drag it above or below another layer.

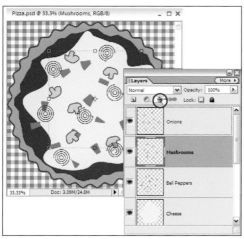

If you decide against putting mushrooms on the pizza, just throw that layer away.

DELETING A LAYER

To delete an unwanted layer, select it and drag it onto the Trash icon 🗑 located at the top of the Layers palette. (Version 3.0 users will find the Trash icon at the bottom of the palette).

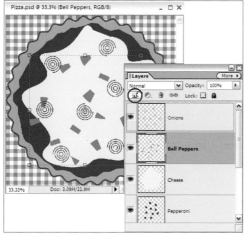

Add extra peppers by duplicating the Bell Peppers layer.

DUPLICATING A LAYER

To duplicate a layer, select and drag it on to the New Layer icon 🗋 located at the top of the Layers palette. (Version 3.0 users will find the New Layer icon at the bottom of the palette).

When you duplicate a layer, all objects on both layers will be in the exact same position, until you reposition and/or edit one of the layers.

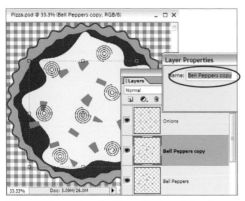

Name a layer by double+clicking it in the Layers palette.

NAMING LAYERS

It's a good habit to give descriptive names to your layers as you create them, especially if it's difficult to identify what's on a layer by looking at the thumbnail, i.e., small objects or similar objects from duplicate layers. To name a layer, either double+click the thumbnail or double+click the name of the layer and type in a new name.

Scale objects on a layer by dragging a corner point of the bounding box. Press Shift to keep it in proportion.

SCALING AND ROTATING LAYER ELEMENTS

When you select the Move tool in the toolbox and then activate a layer, the object(s) on that layer will display a bounding box around the artwork in the document window. The bounding box enables you to quickly scale or rotate the artwork on that layer. This is known as a "transformation edit."

To scale an object, press the Shift key and drag a corner point. Holding down the Shift key while dragging will scale the artwork in proportion. Press Enter to apply the transformation; press Escape (Esc) to cancel the transformation.

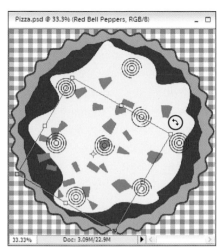

Rotate objects on a layer when you see your cursor turn into a curved arrows icon. Drag in the desired direction.

To rotate an object, hold your cursor a short distance away from a corner point. When the curved arrows appear as your cursor, click and drag to rotate in the direction you wish.

Link layers together when you want to move or transform them at the same time.

LINKING MULTIPLE LAYERS

If you want to move or transform more than one layer at a time, Shift+click the layers in the Layers palette to select them. To keep the layers linked, in case you want to work with them later without having to reselect each one, click the link (chain) icon located at the top of the Layers palette. A link icon will appear next to the layer names. To unlink them, again click the link icon located at the top of the Layers palette.

(Version 3.0 users will find linking capabilities in the column to the left of the layer thumbnails.)

Note the different Color Adjustment commands.

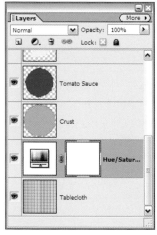

The Hue/Saturation command applied only to the Tablecloth layer in an Adjustment layer.

It's now a purple tablecloth.

USING ADJUSTMENT LAYERS

When you want to make tonal adjustments or color corrections, create an Adjustment layer. They are ideal for experimenting, because the adjustments you make to an image reside on the Adjustment layer and don't affect the actual image pixels until you merge the layers or flatten the image. Adjustment layers give you flexibility because you can edit them at any time or discard them if you don't want to apply your changes.

When you create an Adjustment layer, the adjustment you make is applied to all of the layers below it, unless you create a Clipping Group. When you create a Clipping Group, the adjustment applies only to the layer directly below it. With the Adjustment layer selected, create a Clipping Group by choosing Layer > Group with Previous.

MANAGING LAYERED IMAGES

The more layers you have in an image, the larger the file size. If you want to conserve disk space or you notice Elements behaving sluggishly, consider merging layers to simplify your image and reduce the file size.

MERGING LAYERS

When you choose to merge layers together, Elements no longer needs to keep track of every pixel in the document, so the pixels that you can't see in your composite image are discarded. This ultimately reduces the file size. When you choose Merge Visible from the Layer menu, all layers that are hidden will not be merged. This is the safest choice because there is less of a chance of inadvertently merging layers since you can visually check both your image and the Layers palette.

The Merge Down option, also available in the Layer menu, is used when you want to merge the active (highlighted) layer with the layer directly beneath it.

CAUTION *Keep in mind that you want to merge layers only if you are positive that you will never want to edit those individual layers in the future. The first time you learn this lesson is usually the last.*

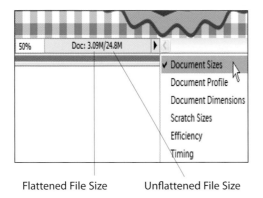

Flattened File Size   Unflattened File Size

FLATTENING AN IMAGE

When you flatten an image, all visible layers are merged into one layer and any layers that are hidden are discarded. It's necessary to flatten an image if the file needs to be saved in a format other than the native Photoshop (.psd) file format for use with other software applications such as Web, desktop publishing, or presentations.

To compare the working file size and the ultimate flattened file size, open the pop-up menu at the bottom of your work area by clicking on the arrow and choosing Document Sizes. The number listed on the left indicates the size of the document when its layers are flattened. The number on the right indicates the size of the working document before it is flattened, when the individual layers are still intact.

Before flattening an image, make sure that all the layers to be included are visible, that is, the Eye icon next to each layer in the Layers palette is turned on. Choose Flatten Image from the Layer Menu.

TIP *Before creating a flattened version, make it a habit to always save a copy of the file unflattened, and named with the .psd (Photoshop Document) extension.*

WORKING WITH SELECTIONS

You create selections when you want to isolate specific areas of an image either to silhouette, color correct, or apply a special effect to that particular area. Anything within the confines of an active selection, often referred to as the "marching ants," can be manipulated without affecting the area outside of the selection. This chapter will guide you in choosing the correct selection tool to use for the task at hand, as well as provide you with a few tips the pros use in making selections. You can practice with many of the images in this chapter by downloading them from the www.photoshopcrafts.com Web site.

The Marquee tools.

THE MARQUEE TOOLS

Use the Rectangular Marquee tool when you want to make a square or rectangular selection. Use the Elliptical Marquee tool when you want to make a circular or oval selection. With either of these tools, if you press the Shift key while dragging, you will constrain the selection to a perfect square or perfect circle.

The "marching ants" indicate an active selection.

THE RECTANGULAR MARQUEE TOOL

Open an image that you can practice with. Press M on your keyboard to select the Rectangular Marquee tool 🔲 (M toggles between the Rectangular Marquee and the Elliptical Marquee tools).

Click and drag a marquee over a portion of the image. When you release your mouse button, the "marching ants" appear.

Now just the border area of the image is selected.

CHOOSING THE INVERSE OF A SELECTION

Very often, you will find in your Photoshop Elements work that it's faster and easier to first select the opposite of what you want. You select the opposite, and then choose Inverse from the Select menu.

Shown at left, selecting Inverse will make the selection act as a border, which can then be manipulated without affecting the center portion of the image.

The higher the Opacity setting, the more "ghosted" the selected area.

A simple stroke can be created when you have an active selection.

GHOSTING A SELECTION

To ghost the selected area, choose Edit > Fill Selection and then choose White from the Contents > Use menu, change the Opacity to 75%, and then click OK. Only the border selection is ghosted.

STROKING A SELECTION

With the ants still marching, you can create a stroke around the artwork by choosing Edit > Stroke Selection. Choose a stroke value, and then click OK.

DESELECTING A SELECTION

When you're finished working with your selection and ready to move on to another task, choose Select > Deselect, or press Ctrl+D on your keyboard.

The original photograph.

Leave areas outside the selection so the feathering will have pixels to work with for the vignette.

That's hot.

THE ELLIPTICAL MARQUEE TOOL

The Elliptical Marquee tool ⬭ enables you to make circular selections. Open a photo that you can practice with and press M to toggle between the Rectangular Marquee tool and the Elliptical Marquee tool. This is the tool to use to make a classic vignette: a photo in a circle or oval with soft, feathered edges. Wedding photographers love a good vignette. Click and drag a marquee over a portion of the image. To start your selection from the center of what you want to select, click in the center, begin dragging and then press the Alt Key. When you release your mouse button, the "marching ants" appear. If necessary, use the arrow keys on your keyboard to "nudge" the selection exactly where you want it.

FEATHER A SELECTION

Choose Select > Feather and enter a value for pixel width. The value will depend on how much softness you want to add to the edge of the image. Click OK.

Select Inverse from the Select menus in order to selected the opposite area. Choose Edit > Fill Selection, and choose White. Click OK. Press Ctrl+D to deselect.

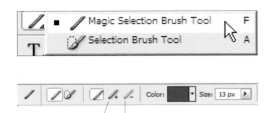

Add to a selection

Subtract from a selection

THE MAGIC SELECTION BRUSH TOOL

Use the Magic Selection Brush tool ✐ to create a selection based on areas of an image where you click, draw, or scribble.

If after your first click or scribble, the Magic Selection Brush tool didn't select everything you intended, you can add to the selection by choosing the Indicate Foreground tool (the Magic Selection Brush tool with the "+") in the Options bar which is located at the top of your work area. Click on the area you want included.

If too much of an area is selected, choose the Indicate Background tool, (the Magic Selection Brush tool with the "-" also in the Options bar, and click on the area you don't want included.

A quick scribble over various pixel colors.

If you need to change the color you click or scribble with in case the default color, red, is too close to the colors in your image, just click on the swatch in the Options bar to open the Color Picker. Click on a color in the Color Field and then click OK.

A very nice selection, indeed.

You can also change the size of the brush in the Options bar, in case you want to draw an outline around the subject rather than click or scribble.

Make a quick selection of the pixels that weren't originally selected by pressing the Shift key and encircling them with the Lasso tool.

The Polygon Lasso tool works well with selections that have straight lines.

THE LASSO TOOLS

Elements has three Lasso tools: the standard Lasso, the Polygon Lasso, and the Magnetic Lasso. Each offers a great deal of flexibility in how you create selections. They are often used in conjunction with the other selection tools.

THE STANDARD LASSO TOOL

The standard Lasso tool is a freehand drawing tool. In the example shown at left, it's used to refine the selection: Press the Shift key and drag to add areas that weren't originally selected by a different selection tool. A "+" sign appears next to your cursor, indicating that you will be adding to the current selection. You must be sure to close the shape you draw by overlapping where you started drawing, otherwise Elements will complete the shape for you by drawing a straight line between where you started and where you ended drawing the shape. If you want to remove an area of a selection, press the Alt key and draw around the area you don't want included in the selection.

THE POLYGON LASSO TOOL

The Polygon Lasso tool is handy when you are selecting a subject with horizontal and vertical lines. Click once to add a point, release the mouse button, and then click again to continue tracing around the subject. If you encounter curves along your path, press the Alt key and drag. Release the Alt key when you need to trace straight lines again. To finish the selection, double+click the point where you began (a circle will appear next to your cursor, indicating that you are closing the selection).

Trace around the subject.

A very nice selection.

Experiment with the color.

Now that's hot pink!

THE MAGNETIC LASSO TOOL

Similar to the Polygon Lasso tool, the Magnetic Lasso tool also works by laying points on a path, but it does it for you automatically, based on the contrast of the subject you are selecting against its background. Click once and trace with your cursor along the edge of what you are selecting. If, at some point, the tool isn't adhering to exactly where you want it to, you can back track your mouse along the path, click to plant your own point and then continue. You can also press the Delete Key to remove dots. Close the selection when you arrive back to your original point by double+clicking. You should see a circle appear next to your cursor, indicating that you are closing the selection.

APPLYING A COLOR ADJUSTMENT TO A SELECTION

In Elements Standard Edit mode (not Quick Fix mode), and with your selection still active, perform a quick color change of just the area selected by choosing Layer > New Adjustment Layer > Hue/Saturation. Click OK in the New Layer dialog box, and then, in the Hue/Saturation dialog box, adjust the Hue slider. Experiment with the Saturation and Lightness sliders if you'd like. Click OK.

THE MAGIC WAND TOOL

The Magic Wand tool selects areas based on color. The higher the tolerance setting in the Options bar, the more of an area the Magic Wand tool selects when you click in an area. For example, if you want to select a specific color but not the neighboring areas that might be shades lighter or darker, use a low tolerance setting. Experiment by entering 1 in the tolerance field and clicking on an area of your image. Next, enter a midrange number, such as 100, and again click on the image. Finally, try a tolerance setting of 255, the highest tolerance setting, and you'll quickly understand.

One click with the Magic Wand at a tolerance setting of 32.

As with many of the other selection tools, press Shift+click to add areas to your selection, and press Alt+click to deselect areas.

USING THE GROW COMMAND

Depending on the color range of what you are selecting, rather than Shift+clicking several times to complete your selection, choose Grow from the Select menu. The Grow command finds pixels similar in color to what is already selected. The amount that the selection "grows" is based on the tolerance setting in the Options bar: The higher the number, the larger the selection. Again, experiment with a low tolerance setting as well as a high setting.

After the Grow command is applied a few times.

The Similar command applied.

Name your selection in the Save Selection dialog box.

Activate your Saved Selection by choosing Load Selection in the Select menu.

USING THE SIMILAR COMMAND

The Similar command takes the expansion of a selection a step further. In addition to selecting neighboring colors, it searches for similar colors elsewhere in the image. In the image shown at left, the Grow command worked well selecting the larger flower. When the Similar command was applied, it reached out and selected the other purple pixels, so all the flowers were selected.

SAVING AND LOADING A SELECTION

It's always a good idea to save a selection, especially if you've spent a long time working on one and perfecting it. You may need to edit the image and use the selection again at a later date. To save a selection, choose Select > Save Selection, type in a name, and click OK. Keep in mind a selection can only be saved within a PSD file (Photoshop Document file).

The selection is saved within your Elements document and can be activated again by choosing Select > Load Selection, choosing it in the Source menu, and then clicking OK.

FOLDING POSTCARD

Sure, email is a great way to send photos to family and friends, but wouldn't it be more fun to send a hand-written postcard with your photos? With this design, the postcard becomes a keepsake and can easily be displayed on a mantle or desk. You can also use this design for a party invitation or a holiday card. With this project, you will learn how to crop and combine images into one document, and how to duplicate and merge layers.

8-1/2 x 11-inch double-sided matte photo paper, such as Staples Photo Supreme

Craft utility knife

Ruler

Bone scorer

Double-sided removable tape, such as Tombo Mono Removable Adhesive

1 Open three images you would like to include in your postcard. To clearly view all three images simultaneously, choose Window > Images > Tile. Make sure the resolution for each photo is the same by choosing File > Open and then choosing Image > Resize > Image Size for each one. Click OK. (For more information on image resolution, see page 13.)

2 Create a new document by choosing File > New > Blank File. The New dialog box appears. Enter a name in the Name field. Enter 9 inches in the Width field and 4.25 inches in the Height field. Enter the same resolution that your chosen photos have. Choose White for Background Contents. Select RGB for Color Mode. Click OK.

3 Select one of the photos to be the main cover photo and choose Rulers from the View menu or press Shift+Ctrl+R. Reposition it by dragging the lower right-hand corner of the image window. Select the Crop tool ⽥ in the toolbox. In the Options bar located at the top of your work area, enter 6 inches in the Width field and 4.25 inches in the Height field and then enter the same resolution as your image.

4 Drag a marquee over the area of the image you want included in the crop. If necessary, reposition the crop box by dragging inside of it or nudging the marquee using the arrow keys on your keyboard. Click the check mark to apply the crop. Choose Window > Images > Tile.

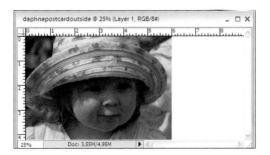

5 Select the Move tool ▶₊ in the tool box, click on the photo and drag it into the blank document. Note that the photo is now on its own layer in the Layers palette. Position the image flush left as shown here.

6 Select your second photo for the cover. This time, change the crop width to 3 inches in the Options bar. Crop the image and position it flush right.

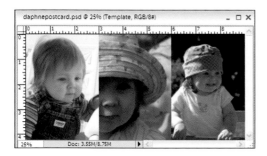

7 Crop the third photo, (the one that will appear inside the card), the same size as the second one, and drag it into the document. Position it flush left.

8 Temporarily hide the first two photos by clicking the Eye icon next to each of the layers in the Layers palette.

9 Create a new layer by clicking on the New Layer icon located at the top of the Layers palette.

10 In the next few steps, you'll design the address area of the postcard. Press D on your keyboard to set your Foreground swatch in the toolbox back to the default black swatch. Press N to select the Pencil tool. In the Options bar, enter 1 pixel in the Size field and 50% in the Opacity field.

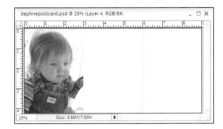

11 Press Shift and drag a vertical line at the 6-inch mark on the ruler.

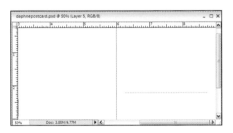

12 Create another new layer by clicking on the New Layer icon located at the top of the Layers palette. Press Shift and drag a horizontal line approximately 2-1/2 inches long starting at the 6-1/4 inch mark on the ruler and approximately two inches from the top of the document.

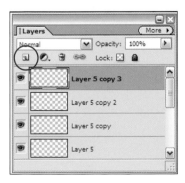

13 Duplicate this layer three times by dragging it on top of the New Layer icon. The duplicate lines are exactly on top of each other, so at this point you'll only see one line, not three. In the next step, you reposition them as address lines.

14 To evenly space out the address lines, Select the Move tool in the toolbox and with the top layer selected, press the down arrow on your keyboard to nudge the line below the others. Repeat this step with the other two layers that contain lines. Pressing Shift while using the nudge keys moves items in 10-pixel increments. Pressing just a nudge key alone moves items in 1-pixel increments.

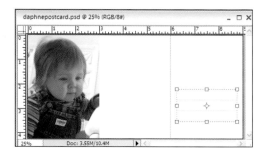

15 Temporarily link the four layers that contain the horizontal lines (don't include the vertical line) by Shift+clicking each layer. You can now reposition all four horizontal lines at the same time using the Move tool or your nudge keys.

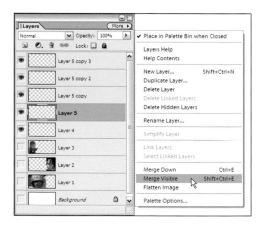

16 Next, hide all of the layers except all five layers that contain the lines by clicking on the Eye icon next to the image layers and Background in the Layers palette. Select Merge Visible from the Layers Palette menu.

17 Choose File > Save. To print the cover of the postcard, make visible those two layers that contain the cover photos. Hide the layers that contain the lines and the inside photo. Choose File > Print.

18 Specify the following settings in your Print dialog boxes:

- Paper Size: 8-1/2 x 11

- Orientation: Landscape

- Media Type: Matte Paper - Heavy

- Print Quality: 720 dpi

- Print Area: Standard and Centered

- Add Crop marks

19 Allow the print to dry. Hide the cover image layers and reveal the inside image and line layers. Turn the sheet over and feed it in to your printer in the same direction. Again, allow the print to dry. Trim the postcard with a craft utility knife and ruler and then use a bone scorer to score and fold at the three-inch mark.

Write a note on the inside center panel. Place a strip of removable double-stick tape to the inside left flap. Check with your post office for the correct postage amount, and address and mail your postcard.

GINGHAM GIFT BOX

Make your next gift stand out with this adorable little pocketbook design. It's a special way to package a pair of earrings, a necklace, or other small gift. You could even design it to hold wedding or baby shower favors. With this project, you will learn how to create the gingham pattern, work with the template, and assemble the pocketbook. You can download the template from the www.photoshopcrafts.com Web site or work with the one included on page 150.

8-1/2 x 11-inch matte or glossy card stock

Craft utility knife

Bone scorer

Craft glue, such as Elmer's

1/4-inch ribbon for the pocketbook strap

1/8-inch hole punch

5/8-inch Velcro dots for the pocketbook closure

Decorative craft punch for embellishment

Mini brad

1 Create a new document by choosing File > New > Blank File. The New dialog box appears. In the Name field, enter "ginghamgiftbox". Enter 8.5 inches in the Width field and 11 inches in the Height field or choose Letter from the Preset pop-up menu. Enter 150 in the Resolution field and choose White for Background Contents. Select RGB for Color Mode. Click OK.

2 Magnify the document by high-lighting the number in the lower left corner of the document window. Enter 300 and press Enter.

3 Click the Foreground swatch at the bottom of the toolbox to display the Color Picker. Drag the triangles up and down the Color Slider to change the range of colors in the Color Field. Click on a color of your choice in the Color Field. Click OK.

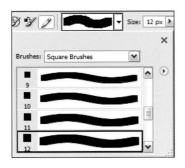

4 Select the Pencil tool 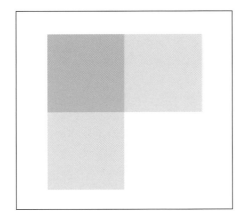 in the toolbox, by selecting and holding on the Brush tool or by typing N. From the Options bar, located at the top of your work area, select Square Brushes from the Brush pop-up menu. Enter 12 pixels in the Size field and press Enter.

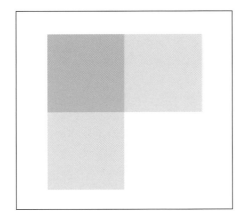

5 With the Pencil tool still selected, click once anywhere on your canvas. A square will appear. Next, change the Opacity setting to 50 percent in the Options bar, then click once to the right and once below the first square to create two new squares. You can choose Edit > Undo or press Ctrl+Z if your second and third squares don't line up properly, and then recreate them.

TIP *To zoom in on your work for a more precise view, press the Z key on your keyboard. Click the magnifying tool a few times in the center of the document. To reactivate the Pencil tool, press N.*

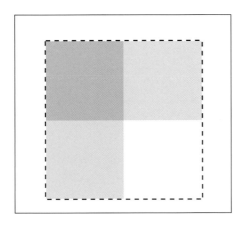

6 Select the Rectangular Marquee tool, then drag a square around the four quadrants, including the lower right area, which represents the white square of the gingham pattern. Select only the area of the squares, not outside "air." This selection defines what will be included in your pattern.

7 Choose Edit > Define Pattern from Selection and enter a name. Click OK. Your pattern is now saved in the Custom Pattern menu. Deselect the art by choosing Select > Deselect or press Ctrl+D.

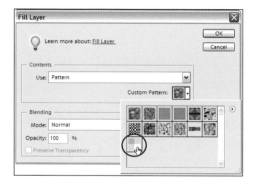

8 Next, choose Edit > Fill Layer > Pattern. Under Contents, choose Pattern from the Use menu, then open the Custom Pattern menu and select your pattern. Click OK. Note that the Background of your document is filled with the gingham pattern. Choose File > Save or press Ctrl+S.

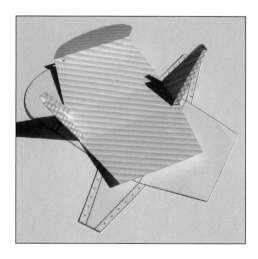

9 Print the pattern on matte or glossy card stock. Allow the print to dry completely. Download the ginghamgiftboxtemplate.pdf from the www.photoshopcrafts Web site and print it out, or make a copy of the one on page 150 and enlarge it 134% to fit an 8-1/2 x 11-inch page. Tape it on top of your patterned sheet. Score the dotted lines using a bone scorer and ruler, then cut on the solid lines with a craft utility knife. Punch holes for the strap and then glue the sides.

10 Knot the ribbon at one end and thread it through one of the holes from the inside and then through the other hole. Trim the ribbon to the length you like and knot it. Use the decorative punch to cut out the flower (or other shape you've chosen) and attach it with a mini brad to the front flap of the pocketbook. Place the Velcro dots at the closure, inside of the pocketbook flap.

TIP *To create the striped pattern for the interior of the pocketbook, follow the same steps as for the gingham pattern, but place the three colored squares in a row.*

ANNIVERSARY VOTIVE

Celebrate a momentous occasion such as a silver or gold wedding anniversary with original photographs illuminated on glass votive holders. You can apply the inkjet decal directly to the glass, or print the image on glossy photo stock and wrap the paper around the candle holder as a sheath, securing the ends with double-sided tape. With this project, you will learn how to create a false duotone effect using the Hue Saturation command.

STUFF YOU WILL NEED

Glass votive holder

Craft utility knife

Ruler

Inkjet decal paper, such as Lazertran

Medium-size bowl of warm water

Rubber squeegee or sponge

Oil-based varnish, such as polyurethane

1 Open the image you want to use for the votive. You'll need a photo with plenty of horizontal image area. Make sure it's in RGB mode by choosing Image > Mode > RGB Color. Measure the height and diameter of the votive holder.

2 Select the Crop tool ⬚, and enter the measurements for Width (the diameter of the votive holder) plus 1/4˝ for overlap, and Height of the holder in the Options bar located at the top of your work area. Press Enter to apply the crop.

3 Drag a marquee over the area of the image you want included in the crop. If necessary, reposition the crop box by dragging inside of it or nudging the marquee using the arrow keys on your keyboard. Click the check mark to apply the crop.

4 To create the false duotone effect, select Enhance > Adjust Color > Adjust Hue/Saturation. Check the Colorize box. Drag the Hue Slider to the desired color and make Saturation and Lightness adjustments if needed. Click OK.

5 Print the artwork on to the smooth, creamy white, eggshell side (not the blue tinted side) of the Lazertran inkjet decal paper. Choose File > Page Setup, select Printer in the dialog box, and then click on Properties.

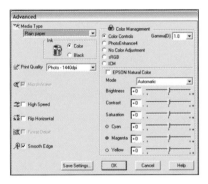

Select Plain Paper for Media type, 1440 dpi for Print Quality, and uncheck High Speed. Click OK. These are the settings that work best for an Epson printer according to Lazertran. If you have an HP printer, "Draft" should be a good setting. For more information about printer settings, visit the Lazertran Web site (www.Lazertran.com) or your printer manufacturer's Web site.

6 Allow the print to dry for at least 30 minutes. With a ruler and craft utility knife, trim the image. Soak the decal in fairly warm water for about 15 seconds (it will curl). Carefully slide the decal off of the backing sheet and onto the glass. Gently position it in place. Carefully remove any air bubbles with your fingertips. The decal is extremely delicate, so use a light touch. Allow the decal to dry overnight and then apply a few coats of oil-based protective varnish.

GARDEN JOURNAL

Give a generic notebook a personal touch, by customizing its cover with your own photographs, simple borders, and a bit of text. I've used a garden theme, but this project is easy to customize for a new baby, a wedding, a summer vacation—whatever the occasion calls for. With this project, you will learn how to work with layers, including creating new layers, reordering, duplicating, and linking them. You will also learn how to choose and apply colors, work with multiple photos, scale artwork, and set text.

6 x 6-inch hardbound spiral notebook

Glossy photo stock

Craft utility knife

Ruler

Spray-mount adhesive

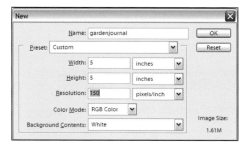

1 Create a new document by choosing File > New. In the Name field enter "gardenjournal". Enter 5 inches in both the Height and the Width fields, and 150 in the Resolution field. Choose RGB for Color Mode and select White for Background Contents. Click OK.

2 Next, choose an overall color for the cover of the document. Click the Foreground swatch 🔲 at the bottom of the Toolbox to display the Color Picker. Drag the triangles up and down the Color Slider to change the range of colors in the Color Field. Click on a color of your choice in the Color Field. Click OK.

3 Choose Edit > Fill Layer and then select Foreground Color from the Contents > Use pop-up list. Make sure Opacity is set to 100 percent and click OK. The layer fills with your selected color.

4 Choose File > Open and select the photograph that you want to use as the main image on the cover of the journal. Position the documents so you can clearly view both of them on your screen. Select the Move tool, and drag the photo into the garden journal document. Note that the photo is now on its own separate layer in the Layers palette.

5 Press Ctrl+T to view the transformation bounding box and then press Ctrl+0 to view the entire document on screen. This will give you access to the transformation handles so you can resize the photo. To adjust the size of the photo while maintaining its proportions, press the Shift key and drag a corner handle. Press Enter to apply the transformation.

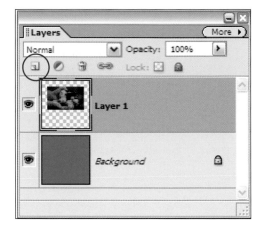

6 Create a new layer by clicking on the New Layer icon located at the top of the Layers palette. This will be the layer that contains the border around the main photo.

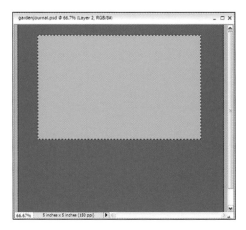

7 Select the Rectangular Marquee tool and drag a rectangle around the photo. Click the Foreground swatch at the bottom of the Toolbox to display the Color Picker. Drag the triangles up and down the Color Slider to change the range of colors in the Color Field. Click on a color of your choice in the Color Field. Click OK.

Fill this selection by choosing Edit > Fill Selection. Choose Deselect from the Select menu or press Ctrl+D. (When you reorder the layers in the next step, the box will appear as a border underneath the image.)

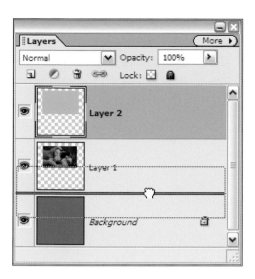

8 Change the order of the layers by dragging Layer 2 below Layer 1 in the Layers palette. When a line appears between Layer 1 and the Background, release the mouse button. Resize the border on Layer 2 if needed, by dragging the corner points, again maintaining proportions by pressing the Shift key.

TIP *To keep organized, you may want to name the layers in the Layers palette. Just double+click on a Layer thumbnail, type in a descriptive name, and click OK.*

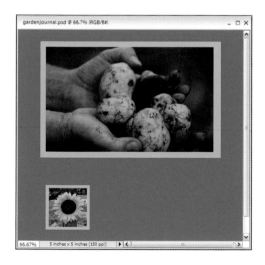

9 Open another photo and, with the Move tool selected, drag it into the garden journal document. Repeat steps 5 through 7 to create a smaller border, and then adjust the order of the layers so the border square is beneath the corresponding image.

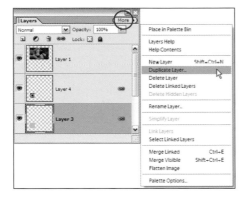

10 Before adding the next two photos to the cover, duplicate the smaller border layer twice, by clicking the More button at the top of the Layers palette and selecting Duplicate Layer. With the Move tool, position the borders.

TIP *To duplicate a layer, drag it onto the New Layer icon at the top of the Layers palette.*

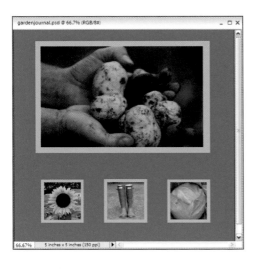

11 Open two more photos and drag them into the garden journal document. Resize them and place them over the borders.

TIP *To move a photo and its corresponding border together, link the layers by first Shift+clicking the two layers, and then clicking on the Link icon located at the top of the Layers palette. To unlink the layers, select one of them, and click once again on the Link icon at the top of the palette.*

12 Select the Horizontal Type tool T in the Toolbox, then click anywhere in the document. Type the title for your journal. Click and drag over the text to highlight it, and choose your formatting in the Options bar located at the top of your work area. I selected Avenir.

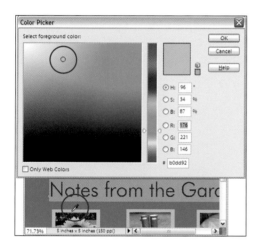

13 With the text still highlighted, change the color by opening the Color Picker. Either pick a color in the Color Field, or float your cursor over different areas of your photo. Your cursor will change into an Eyedropper ✐, enabling you to sample a specific color in your image. Click on the desired color and then click OK. Reposition the text with the Move tool, if necessary. Choose File > Save or press Ctrl+S.

TIP *With the Move tool selected, use the arrow keys on your keyboard to nudge layer elements into their desired positions.*

14 Print your artwork on a premium photo stock. Make sure you allow the print to dry before proceeding. Trim the artwork with a craft utility knife and a ruler. In a well-ventilated area, spray the back of the print with spray adhesive, and mount your art on to the cover of the journal.

"WE LOVE GRANDMA" APRON

*Could there be a grandmother anywhere who wouldn't love to receive this apron as a gift?
I can imagine this worn at every Thanksgiving for years to come. With this project, you
will learn how to combine images into one document, scale and rotate images, sample
colors with the Eyedropper tool, and create borders.*

1 Choose a group of your favorite family photos for your apron design. Create a new document by choosing File > New > Blank File. The New dialog box appears. Enter a name in the Name field. Enter 8″ x 8″ in the Height and the Width fields. Enter the resolution of your chosen photos. (For more information on Image resolution, see page 13.) Choose White for Background Contents. Select RGB for Color Mode. Click OK.

2 Open the first photo and position it next to the blank document so you can see both on screen. The easiest way to do this is to choose Window > Images > Tile. With the photo as the active document, select the Move tool ✛ in the toolbox, or press V on your keyboard. Drag the photo into the blank document.

TIP *When you drag and drop an image from one document to another, Photoshop Elements makes a copy of the image and your original remains intact.*

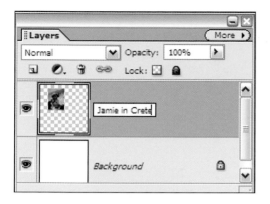

3 The layer containing the photo is now on top of the Background and is automatically named Layer 1. To keep your document organized, give each layer a descriptive name as you work. Double+click on the default name of the layer in the Layers palette and enter a name.

4 Select the Move tool in the toolbox, and while holding down the Shift key, click and drag a corner point to resize the image to your liking. Pressing the Shift key while you drag will resize the image proportionately. I made my images approximately two inches wide. It's helpful to have the Info palette open as you resize your images (Window > Info). It actively displays the width and height of your image as you resize it. Press Enter on your keyboard to apply the transformation.

5 To create the frame for the photo, choose a complimentary color by sampling a color that exists in the photo with the Eyedropper tool ✐. Select the Eyedropper tool by pressing I on your keyboard. Click anywhere in the photo. Note the color you sampled is now your Foreground color in the toolbox.

6 Choose Edit > Stroke (Outline) Selection. Enter a Stroke Width and check Inside for Location. (You'll get slightly rounded corners if you choose Outside or Centered for Location.) The Blending Mode should be set to Normal and the Opacity set to 100 percent. Click OK.

7 With the Move tool, position your cursor just outside of the art until it displays curved arrows. Rotate the image by clicking and dragging in the desired direction. Pressing the Shift key while you drag will constrain the rotation to 45° increments. Press Enter to apply the rotation.

TIP *If you find all of a sudden that you can't select a different layer, or create a new layer, or bring in another image, it might be because you forgot to apply the transformation (scaling or rotating) to your image. Remember to press the Enter key to apply the transformation or the Esc key to cancel it.*

8 Repeat steps 2 through 7 with the remaining photos and resize, rotate and position them as you like.

9 Select the top layer in the Layers palette and then scroll down to the bottom of the palette and Shift+click the bottom layer (not the Background) to select all the image layers. Click the link icon at the top of the Layers palette, to link the layers together.

Choose Rulers from the View Menu and then press Ctrl+T and resize the linked images to measure approximately six inches.

10 When you are ready to print the image using the transfer paper, follow the manufacturer directions and don't forget to flip the layout, in order to print it correctly once ironed on to the fabric. Choose Image > Rotate > Flip Horizontal (not Flip Layer Horizontal). If you flip the artwork in Elements, don't choose the option again in the Page Setup in the printing options.

PET PLACE MAT

Your furry friend will certainly enjoy breakfast with this easy-to-make. decorative place mat. Your local craft store carries a wide variety of decorative papers that you can mix and match to create the look you want. With this project, you will learn how to silhouette an image, work with layers, and create a border. You will need to scan the decorative papers and then take your final print to the local copy shop and have it laminated (between $3 and $7).

STUFF YOU WILL NEED

Decorative paper

11″ x 17″ glossy photo stock

Laminate

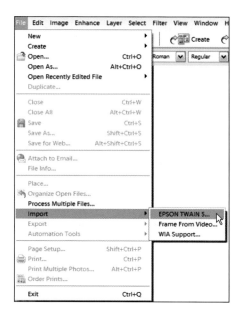

1 Scan the decorative paper that you will use for the background. Select File > Import and choose your scanner model from the menu. If it's not listed, follow your scanner manufacturer instructions to install the necessary software. Use a resolution setting of 150 ppi. The image will automatically open in Photoshop Elements.

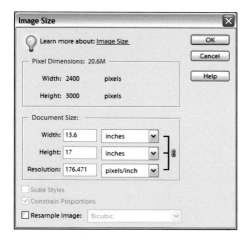

2 Choose Image > Resize > Image Size and enter 17 inches in the Height field. Let Photoshop Elements automatically set the value for the width.

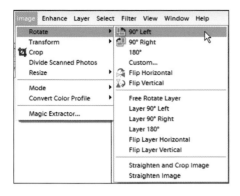

3 If necessary for your design, rotate the canvas by choosing Image > Rotate > 90° (Left or Right, as appropriate). Click OK.

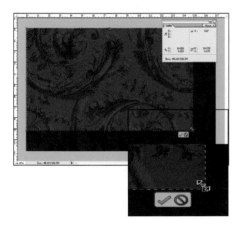

4 Choose Show Rulers from the View menu or press Shift+Ctrl+R. This will help you measure while using the Crop tool. Select the Crop tool ⛏ in the toolbox, or press C on your keyboard. Click, drag and measure to the size of 11″ x 17″. It can also be helpful to open the Info palette (Window > Info) to assist with accurate measurement. If necessary, reposition the marquee by dragging inside of it or dragging on the side and corner points. Click the check mark to apply the crop.

5 Scan your next sheet of decorative paper for use in the interior of the place mat. Rotate the image if needed, by choosing Edit > Rotate.

With the Move tool ▸₊, drag the inset image into the background document. Center and scale it, if needed, by pressing the Shift key and dragging on a corner point.

6 Next, open the image of the pet that you want to silhouette and add to the place mat. Keep in mind, it's easier to silhouette a subject if it's been photographed against a neutral background.

7 Select the Magic Wand tool in the toolbox and click once on the background area of the image. To continue adding to the selection, press the Shift key and click another area of the background. Continue adding areas to the selection.

8 If you have tiny blinking areas that are not part of the selection, switch to the Lasso tool 〰. Continue to press the Shift key and click and drag around the blinking area to add to the selection.

9 If you have inadvertently picked up areas of the subject in your selection, press the Alt key and remove that area of the selection by dragging a circle around it.

10 Next, since you ultimately want the subject selected (not the background), you need to select the inverse of the selected area by choosing Select > Inverse. Now the subject is selected.

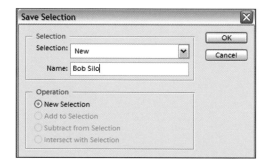

11 After all that work making the selection, it's time to save it within the document, in case you need to improve it or use it again. Choose Select > Save Selection, and enter a name. Click OK.

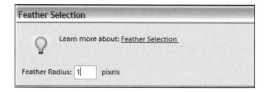

12 Before dropping the selection into the place mat document, it's important to soften the edges so it doesn't appear as if it's cut and pasted on top of a different background. To soften the edges of the selection, choose Select > Feather and enter a value of 1. Click OK.

13 Select the Move tool, and drag and drop the selection into the background image. Note that it is now on its own layer in the Layers palette. Position it where you wish.

14 Click and drag on a corner point while pressing the Shift key, if you need to scale the image.

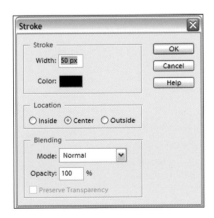

15 To add a border to the inset scanned paper image, select that Layer in the Layers palette and choose Edit > Stroke (Outline) Selection. Enter a value in the Width field. Click on the color swatch to open the Color Picker, then click in the Color Field on the left side of the dialog box to choose a color. Click OK to exit the Color Picker. Make sure Opacity is set to 100 percent in the Stroke dialog box and click OK.

16 The next step is to add text to the image. Select the Text tool **T** in the toolbox and click anywhere in the document. Type what you would like and highlight the text. Choose a font and a size in the Options bar, located at the top of the work area. (I chose Scriptina at 485 points.) If you would like to change the color of the text, click on the color swatch in the Options bar to open the Color Picker. Use the Move tool to place the text where you want it.

TIP *The Scriptina font is available free at www.desktoppub.about.com.*

17 The final step before printing and laminating the place mat is to flatten the image into one layer. This will substantially reduce the file size. You can track the file size of an image in the Status Bar located at the bottom of your document. Click on the triangle and choose Document Sizes. The number on the right indicates the file size with all layers intact and unflattened. The number on the left indicates the size of the file after it is flattened.

CAUTION *Be sure you really want to flatten the image before you do so, since you will no longer be able to edit individual layers. It's always wise to save a copy of the file unflattened and named with the .psd (Photoshop Document) extension. See page 24 for more information.*

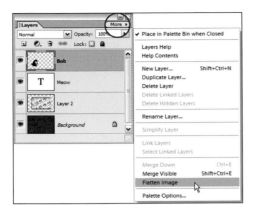

18 In the Layers palette, click the More button and choose Flatten Image. Choose File > Save or press Ctrl+S.

Print the image on glossy photo stock and allow it to dry completely before laminating.

BLACKBERRY PRESERVES LABEL

I love the tulip-shaped canning jars by the German company, Weck. They are so much prettier and more unique than the everyday Mason jar. Visit www.weckcanning.com to see the unique jars the company offers. If you want to use the blackberry photo for your label, you can download it from www.photoshopcrafts.com. With this project, you will learn how to create the label border with a custom pattern, use the Magic Wand tool to create a silhouette, set text, and print multiple images on one sheet.

8-1/2 x 11-inch glossy photo stock

1/4-inch ribbon

1/8-inch hole punch

Craft utility knife

Ruler

1 Open the photo you plan to put on the label. In this example, I shot blackberries with mint leaves on a white background to make silhouetting easy.

Press I on your keyboard to select the Eyedropper tool 🖋, and click a color in the image that you want to use in the border design. A second color for the border will be chosen later.

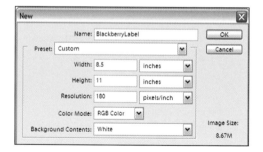

2 Create a new document by choosing File > New > Blank File. The New dialog box appears. Enter a name in the Name field. Choose Letter from the Preset pop-up menu. Enter the resolution of the photo.

To learn the resolution of an image, choose File > Open, and then choose Image > Resize > Image Size. Note the resolution, then click Cancel to close the dialog box.

Choose White for Background Contents. Select RGB for Color Mode. Click OK.

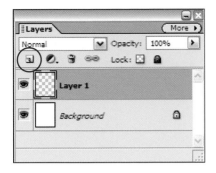

3 Create a new layer, by clicking on the New Layer icon located at the top of the Layers palette. Your new layer is named "Layer 1".

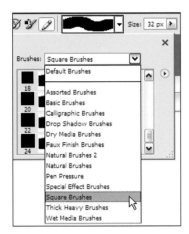

4 Press Ctrl + a few times to zoom in on your document. Select the Pencil tool ✏ in the toolbox, by pressing N on your keyboard. In the Options bar located at the top of your work area, select Square Brushes from the Brushes menu and enter 32 pixels in the Size field.

If you're working with an image at a lower or higher resolution than 180, you need to adapt the brush size. For example, if your image resolution is 72 ppi, enter a brush size of 15 pixels. If your image resolution is 300 ppi, enter a pixel diameter of 60.

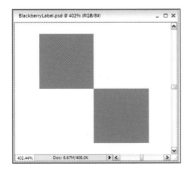

5 Click once with the Pencil tool anywhere on the canvas. Click again on a diagonal line, in the lower right area.

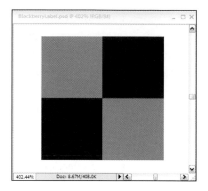

6 Go back to the photo and select another, contrasting color using the Eyedropper tool. Switch to your other document and add two more squares with the new color, as shown here.

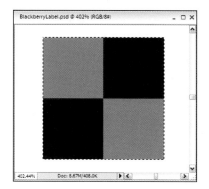

7 The next step is to create a pattern using the four squares. Select the Rectangular Marquee tool □ and drag a marquee around the squares. Select only the area of the squares, not outside "air." This selection defines what will be included in your pattern. You must use the Rectangular Marquee tool (not the Magic Wand tool or other selection tool).

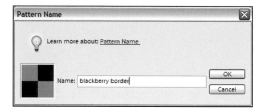

8 Next, choose Edit > Define Pattern from Selection. Enter a name for your custom pattern and click OK. Deselect the artwork by pressing Ctrl+D.

Now that your pattern is stored in the Custom Patterns palette, you can delete the original art. Press D to set the Foreground and Background swatches back to the default setting. Press Ctrl+Backspace. This will fill the layer with white, which is the Background swatch color.

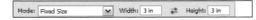

9 Press Ctrl+0 to fit your canvas on screen. Select the Rectangular Marquee tool in the toolbox and, in the Options bar, located at the top of your work area, select Fixed Size from the Mode menu. Enter 3 inches in both the Height and the Width fields and then click on your canvas. Click once on the canvas to create a square selection.

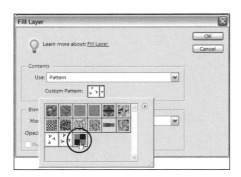

10 Choose Edit > Fill Selection. Choose Pattern from the Contents > Use menu, then open the Custom Pattern menu and click on your pattern. Click OK. Note that your active selection is filled with the pattern. Press Ctrl+D to deselect.

11 The next step is to do a quick clean-up on the edges of the pattern, since you will ultimately use just one row of squares as the border and delete the interior area. (Patterns don't always fill selections exactly as you expect them to.)

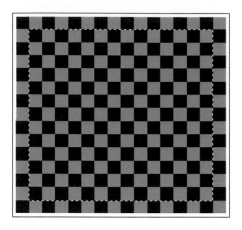

12 Make sure Mode is set to Normal in the Options bar, for the Rectangular Marquee tool. Make a Selection as shown at left so no partial squares are in the selection. Zoom in on your artwork, if needed.

Select Inverse from the Select menu. Press the Delete key and then press Ctrl+D to deselect. Change the Mode back to Normal in the Options bar.

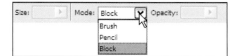

13 It's quite possible that you may need to further clean up the border depending on how accurately you placed your selection. Once again, zoom in on the artwork. Select the Eraser tool ✐ in the toolbox, and set the Mode to Block in the Options bar.

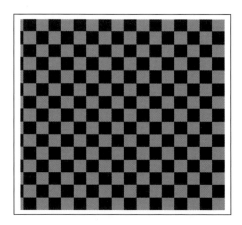

14 Press the Shift key and drag along each edge to remove unwanted pixels, so that each square will be perfect. Pressing the Shift key while you drag will erase the pixels in a straight line. Release the mouse button after removing pixels on each side.

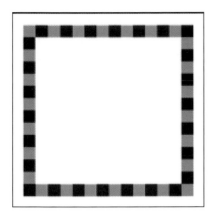

15 Select the Rectangular Marquee tool and drag a selection over the art to include all but the single outermost row of squares. Press Delete. You now have the outer border of the label design. Press Ctrl+D to deselect.

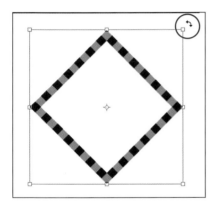

16 Press Ctrl+T to display the transformation bounding box around the border. Hold your cursor outside the bounding box. When the cursor displays curved arrows, press the Shift key and drag. Rotate the box 45°. Press Enter to apply the transformation.

17 Now, it's time to go back to the photo you want to use on the label. I hope you, too, have shot your chosen subject on a white background.

Select the Magic Wand ✎ in the toolbox and click anywhere on the white background of your image. Press Shift and click on other areas of the background that need to be included.

18 Since you ultimately want the subject selected (not the background), you need to select the inverse of the selected area by choosing Select > Inverse. Now the subject is selected. To soften the edges of the selection, choose Select > Feather and enter 1 as a value. Click OK. Save the selection in case you need to use it again by choosing Select > Save Selection. Enter a name and then click OK. Since it's saved in the Elements document, you can call it up at a later date if needed by choosing Select > Load Selection.

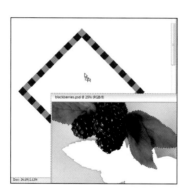

19 Select the Move tool ⊹ and drag the selection into the label document. Place it wherever you like. If you need to scale the image, press the Shift key and drag on a corner handle. Press Enter to apply the transformation.

20 Select the Horizontal Type tool **T** in the toolbox and click anywhere on the canvas. Type in what you want, and then drag over the text to highlight it. Choose a font and size in the Options bar, located at the top of your work area. I chose Scriptina for "Carolyn's", and Trajan for "Blackberry Preserves". Select the Move tool in the toolbox and position the text.

21 Press C on your keyboard to select the Crop tool ⊥. Drag a marquee around your artwork. Adjust the boundaries, if necessary, by dragging the handles of the box. Press Enter to apply the crop.

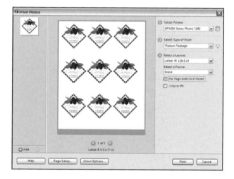

22 If you're planning to make more than a few jars of preserves, obviously you'll want to print more than one label. Choose File > Print Multiple Photos. Choose Picture Package and then check the box for Fill Page With First Photo. From there, you can select how many labels you want printed on the page in the Select a Layout menu.

Print the labels on glossy photo stock and allow the print to dry. Trim the individual labels with a straight-edge ruler and craft utility knife. Punch a hole at the top of the label. Thread ribbon through the hole and around the jar, and attach it by tying a bow.

NEEDLEPOINT PILLOW

Create a canine tapestry using a photo of your very own Fluffy or Fido. With this project, you will learn how to use the Filter Gallery, apply the Dry Brush filter to give your photo a painterly effect, and transfer the image onto needlepoint canvas. From there, the needle-point and sewing work is up to you.

STUFF YOU WILL NEED

8-1/2 x 11-inch inkjet transfer paper for fabric, such as Lazertran Textile

Needlepoint materials including canvas, tapestry yarn, needle

Sewing materials including pillow form, fabric, trim, thread

1 Open the photo you want to use for the needlepoint pillow. You will be simplifying the image (think of a paint by number). An image with contrasting areas works best. Decide how large you want the needlepoint area to be, and ultimately how large the finished pillow will be. Also, you should purchase the needlepoint canvas 1 - 2 inches larger than the image size you've chosen.

2 Crop the image if needed, by selecting the Crop tool 🔲 in the toolbox or by pressing C on your keyboard.

Drag a marquee over the area of the image you want included in the crop. If necessary, reposition the crop box by dragging inside of it or nudging the marquee using the arrow keys on your keyboard. You can also crop the image again by eye, but with the help of the Info palette. Choose Window > Info to open the Info palette. Click the check mark to apply the crop.

If you know exactly what size you want, you can enter the dimensions in the Options bar located at the top of your work area and then drag the marquee and click the check mark to apply the crop.

3 The next step is to apply the Dry Brush filter to not only give the photo a painterly effect, but to lessen the finer details. This will make the needlepoint work easier. The Dry Brush filter also works well on photos intended to be printed on linen canvas.

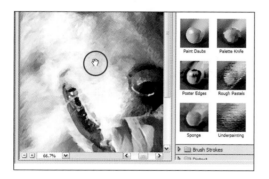

4 Select Filter > Artistic > Dry Brush. The Dry Brush filter dialog box opens in the Filter Gallery. Your cursor has now turned into the Hand tool which enables you to drag and pan to different areas of the image. You can then view how the filter effect is applied to different detailed areas of the image.

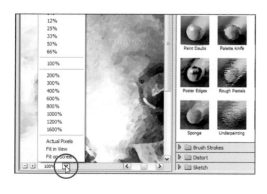

5 Change the viewing size of the image window by clicking on the down arrow located at the bottom of the window.

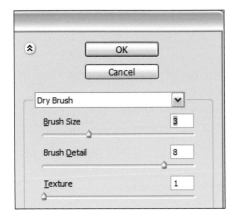

6 Depending on how much detail you have in your image, you will need to experiment with the Brush Size, Brush Detail, and Texture sliders. Remember that you are simplifying the image and you want a paint-by-number effect (less is more).

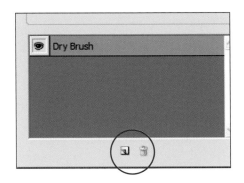

7 You can duplicate the filter effect you're working with to intensify it or apply additional filter effects. To add an additional effect, click on the New Layer Effect icon in the lower right corner of the Gallery window. To delete a filter effect, click on the Trash icon. Click OK to apply the filter effect to your image.

8 When you are ready to print the image onto the transfer paper, follow the directions provided by the transfer paper manufacturer. Remember to flip the image so it prints correctly once it's ironed onto the canvas. Choose Image > Rotate > Flip Horizontal. If you flip the image in Elements, don't choose the option again in the page setup and printing options dialog boxes.

9 Allow the print to dry for at least 30 minutes before proceeding. Trim the image with a craft utility knife and straight-edge ruler. Iron the image onto the canvas following the instructions provided by the transfer paper manufacturer. Be sure to leave one to two inches of blank canvas around your image for handling purposes.

10 Here's an example of the finished needlepoint.

BIRTHDAY BUCKET

Turn an ordinary galvanized bucket into an extraordinary gift. I made this one to celebrate my sister's birthday. Or, how about filling the bucket with spa essentials for a Mother's Day gift, or with small gourmet finds as a hostess gift? With this project you will learn how to easily create the appearance of a black-and-white image while still working in RGB color mode, mask an image inside a shape, use the Warped Text tool, and work with inkjet decal paper.

Galvanized bucket

Inkjet decal paper, such as Lazertran

Craft utility knife or scissors

Medium-size bowl of warm water

Oil-based polyurethane

1 Open the image you would like to use for this project. If it's a color photo and you want to make it appear black and white, choose Enhance > Adjust Color > Remove Color. This method works well when you want to have a black and white photo effect along with color in the same document.

2 Double-click the Background in the Layers palette and enter a name in the New Layer dialog box. Click OK. This turns the Background into a layer which then enables you to place a layer underneath it.

3 Increase the size of the canvas by choosing Image > Resize > Canvas Size. Enter 2″ in the Width and Height fields. Check the Relative box and select the center square of the Anchor diagram. This adds canvas around all four sides of the image. Click OK. The checkerboard pattern now displayed around your image represents transparency.

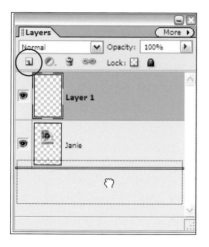

4 Create a new layer by clicking on the New Layer icon located at the top of the Layers palette. Drag the new layer below the other. When a black line appears, release the mouse button. Fill this layer with white by choosing Edit > Fill Layer. Select White from the Contents > Use pop-up menu. Click OK.

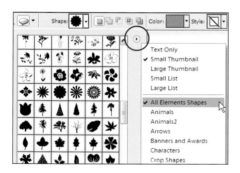

5 Next, select the Custom Shape tool in the toolbox. In the Options bar located at the top of your work area, open the Shapes palette and click the arrow (circled here) to open the palette menu. Select All Elements Shapes.

6 Select a shape, press Shift and drag over the area of the image you want inside the shape. Don't worry if your image is not perfectly centered; you can fix this later. Note you now have a Shape layer in the Layers palette.

7 To mask the image inside the shape, select the image layer and choose Layer > Group with Previous. Note that the image thumbnail in the Layers palette is offset and an arrow points to the layer below. This is called a Clipping Group. To release the image from the mask, select Layer > Ungroup.

TIP *With the Move tool selected, you can easily adjust the position or size of either the image or the mask.*

TIP *Another way to create a Clipping Group is to press the Alt key and click on the line between the two layers in the Layer Palette. A pair of wedding rings appears as your cursor. This is known as "marrying" the layers. Alt+click the line to release the Clipping Group.*

8 Select the Horizontal Type tool **T** in the toolbox, then click anywhere in the document. Type what you would like. Click and drag over the text to highlight it and choose your formatting in the Options bar located at the top of your work area. I selected Fontdinerdotcom. Select the Move tool and position the text.

TIP *The Fontdinerdotcom font is available free at www.fontdiner.com*

9 With the text still highlighted, click the Warped Text button in the Options bar.

10 Experiment with the different options and choose one. Click OK. I chose the Arc style with a Bend setting of +50%.

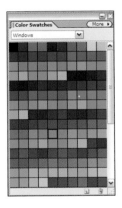

11 Open the Color Swatches palette by choosing Window > Color Swatches.

12 Change the color of each letter by highlighting each one at a time by clicking and dragging over the letter with the Horizontal Text tool **T** and clicking on a swatch in the Color Swatches palette.

13 Choose File > Save to save the project. When you are ready to print on to the inkjet decal paper, follow the directions provided by the transfer paper manufacturer. Allow the print to dry for at least 30 minutes.

With cuticle scissors or a craft utility knife, trim the artwork into separate pieces. Soak the decals one at a time in fairly warm water for about 15 seconds (it will curl). Carefully slide each decal off of the backing sheet and onto the bucket. Gently position each in place. Carefully remove any air bubbles with your fingers. The decal is extremely delicate, so use a light touch.

Allow the decal to dry overnight, and then apply several coats of protective oil-based polyurethane. Keep in mind that areas of the decal intended to be transparent will remain white until you apply the polyurethane.

TRAVEL PHOTO CD COVER

Once you've learned how to organize and manage your digital images with Photoshop Elements, you can create attractive covers for your photo collections. This is a great way to package and share pictures and slide shows of not just your travels, but also pictures of your family. With this project, you will learn how to mask an image inside text, ghost an image by changing its opacity, silhouette an image, and work with custom shapes.

8-1/2 x 11-inch glossy photo stock

1 Open the photo you want to use for the cover of your travel CD.

2 The final trim size for the cover of the CD is 4.75 square inches. Crop your image by selecting the Crop tool ⌗ in the toolbox or by pressing C on your keyboard. If you know exactly what size you want, you can enter the dimensions in the Options bar located at the top of your work area.

3 Drag a marquee over the area of the image you want included in the crop. If necessary, reposition the crop box by dragging inside it, or nudge it by using the arrow keys on your keyboard. Click the check mark to apply the crop, or press Enter on your keyboard.

4 Select the Horizontal Type tool T in the toolbox, then click anywhere in the document. Type the title for your CD. Drag over the text to highlight it, and choose your formatting in the Options bar located at the top of your work area. I selected the font, Textile. Since you will be masking an image inside the text later, the color of the text is irrelevant. However, you do need to select a large, bold display face for optimal legibility of both the type and the image.

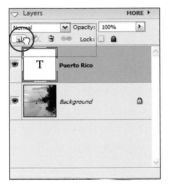

5 The next step is to make a duplicate of the Background. This will be the image layer that will be masked inside the text. Select the Background in the Layers palette and drag it on top of the New Layer icon located at the top of the Layers palette. This layer is now named Background copy.

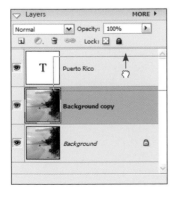

6 Drag the Background copy layer to the top of the stacking order of the Layers palette, above the text layer.

Next, double+click the Background in the Layers palette, leave it named Layer 0, and then click OK. This will enable you to place a layer below it later in the project.

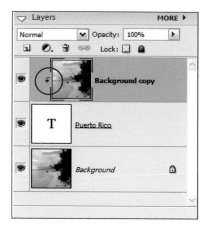

7 To mask the image inside the text, select the Background copy layer and choose Layer > Group with Previous. Note that the image thumbnail in the Layers palette is offset and an arrow points to the layer below. This is called a Clipping Group. You won't see the results of the Clipping Group until Step 11, since there are a few more things you need to do first.

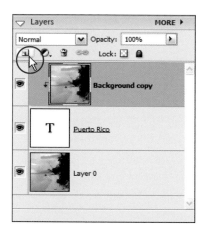

8 Next, create a new blank layer by clicking on the New Layer icon located at the top of the Layers palette.

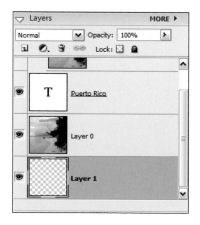

9 Drag Layer 1 to the bottom position in the stacking order of the Layers palette, beneath Layer 0. The checkerboard pattern in the Layer 1 thumbnail means the layer is transparent.

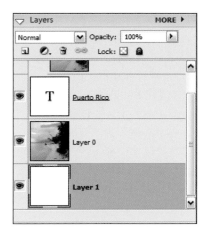

10 The next step is to fill the layer with white so that, when you drop the opacity of the layer above it, you won't see the checkerboard, just the opacity change against the white background. Choose Edit > Fill Layer and then choose White from the Contents > Use pop-up list. Click OK.

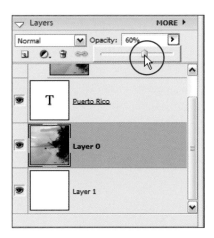

11 Select Layer 0, and then click on the arrow to the right of the Opacity box at the top of the Layers palette to reveal the slider. Drag the Opacity slider in the Layers palette down to 60 percent. You may also highlight the percentage field, enter a number, and press Enter on your keyboard.

12 In this example, lowering the opacity of the background image, also known as "ghosting," makes the text and the imaged masked inside it 'pop,' or become more of a focal point.

13 If you want to resize the text, select the text layer in the Layers palette, and then select the Move tool ▶⊕ in the tool-box. Press and drag on a corner point to scale the Clipping Group.

You may also rotate it by holding your cursor slightly away from the bounding box. When the cursor displays curved arrows, drag in the direction you like. Press the Ctrl key while dragging a middle point in order to skew the artwork. Press Enter to apply the transformation.

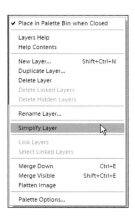

14 The next step is to add a stroke of color around the text, but before you can do that, you need to Simplify the text layer. This means you are converting the vector-based text into a raster, or pixel-based image layer, so that it will no longer be editable. Select the text layer and choose Simplify Layer from the Layers palette pop-up menu.

15 With the Simplified type layer still selected in the Layers palette, Choose Merge Clipping Mask from the Layers palette pop-up menu. Keep in mind that once you merge a Clipping Mask, you won't be able to reposition the image masked inside the text, so be sure you're happy with the way it looks before proceeding.

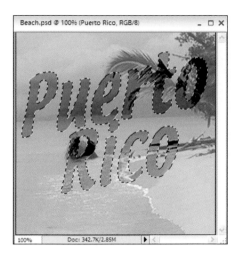

16 Ctrl+click the text layer thumbnail in the Layers palette to create an active selection.

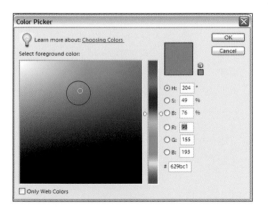

17 Click on the larger Foreground swatch in the toolbox ◼ to open the Color Picker and choose a color for the stroke around the text. Either pick a color in the Color Field, or float your cursor over different areas of your photo. Your cursor will change into an eyedropper ✒, enabling you to sample a specific color in your image. Click on your desired color and then click OK.

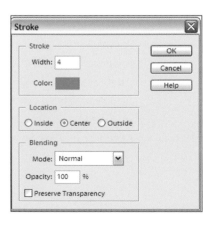

18 Choose Edit > Stroke (Outline) Selection. I chose a stroke of 4 pixels wide, and centered, which means 2 pixels will be on the outside of the "marching ants" and 2 pixels will be on the inside. Click OK to apply the stroke to the selection, and then press Ctrl+D to deselect.

19 Here is what your stroked text should look like.

20 Open the next image that you want to include on the cover of your travel CD, and select the Magnetic Lasso tool 🪢 in the toolbox. Click and trace around the subject. If the Magnetic Lasso tool isn't adhering to the edge the way you want it to, you can click at that location and plant a point, and then continue tracing around the subject. When your cursor gets close to where you started, you will see a little circle beside the cursor icon. This means you are ready to close the path you've drawn and complete your active selection. Click when you see the little circle and your selection appears.

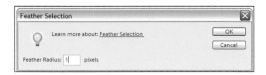

21 Before dragging the sele-
tion into the CD cover
document, it's important to soften the
edges so it doesn't appear as if it were
cut and pasted on top of a different
background. To soften the edges of the
selection, choose Select > Feather and
enter a value of 1. Click OK.

22 Select the Move tool, and drag
the selection into the CD cover
image. Note that it is now on its own
layer in the Layers palette.

23 Scale the image by pressing
the Shift key and dragging
on a corner point of the bounding
box. Press Enter to apply the transformation, and then select the Move tool
to reposition the image.

24 Press D on your keyboard to set the Foreground and Background swatches 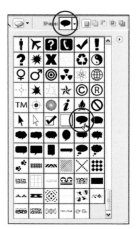 back to the default black and white. Click on the curved arrows next to the swatches in the toolbox, or press X to switch the colors, so white is now the Foreground color.

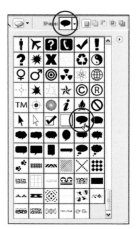

25 Next, add a talk bubble by pressing U on your keyboard, and then selecting the talk bubble icon in the Options bar located at the top of your work area. Open the Shape menu in the Options bar and scroll almost to the bottom of the library, and choose a talk bubble.

26 Drag a talk bubble to make it the size you like. You can flip it around by selecting Image > Rotate > Flip Layer Horizontal. Select the Move tool in the toolbox, and reposition and resize the talk bubble, if necessary. Press Enter to apply the transformation. Drop the opacity to 40 percent by dragging the Opacity slider to the left at the top of the Layers palette.

27 To set text for the talk bubble, first set the Foreground and Background swatches back to default by pressing D on your keyboard. Select the Horizontal Text tool, and choose your formatting in the Options bar located at the top of your work area. I chose Comic Sans. Click anywhere in the document, and type what you would like. With the Move tool, position the text over the talk bubble. Press Enter. Select both the talk bubble layer and the text layer, by Shift+clicking both in the Layers palette to reposition them simultaneously.

28 Add more text to the CD cover if you'd like, and then save the file by pressing Ctrl+S. Print your cover on glossy photo stock, allow it to dry, and then trim it with a straight-edged ruler and craft utility knife.

PARISIAN NUMBER TILES

On a recent trip to Paris, I came across beautiful hand-painted house number tiles in a quaint little shop in the Place du Tertre, a kitchy, touristy shopping area located a few streets away from the Basilique Sacré Coeur. This project is inspired by that visit. But you need not stop at the idea of house number tiles. You may use the techniques shown here to create your own kitchen and bath tiles. In this project, you will primarily learn how to use the Custom Shape tool, the Selection Brush tool, and how to work with inkjet decal paper.

STUFF YOU WILL NEED

4-1⁄2-inch white ceramic tiles

Inkjet decal paper, such as Lazertran

Craft utility knife

Ruler

Medium size bowl of warm water

Oil-based varnish, such as polyurethane

1 Create a new document by choosing File > New > Blank File. In the Name field enter "housenumbers". Enter 11 inches in the Width field and 8.5 inches in the Height field. Enter 150 in the Resolution field and choose White for Background Contents. Select RGB for Color Mode. Click OK.

2 Click the New Layer icon in the Layers palette. This layer will be used only as a template. Name the layer by double+clicking "Layer 1" in the Layers palette and typing the word "template". Press Enter.

3 Select the Rectangular Marquee tool ⬚ in the toolbox, then in the Options bar, choose Fixed Size for Mode. Highlight the Height field and enter 4.25 inches and then highlight the Width field and enter 4.25 px. Click once on your canvas and a rectangular selection appears.

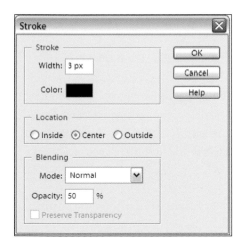

4 Click on the Default Foreground and Background swatches icon ▪ in the Toolbox to set the Foreground color to black and then choose Edit > Stroke (Outline) Selection. Enter 3 pixels for Width, Center, and 50 percent for Opacity. Click OK. Choose Deselect from the Select menu or press Ctrl+D.

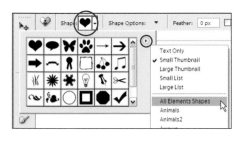

5 Next, select the Custom Shape tool ⬮ in the toolbox. In the Options bar, located at the top of your work area, open the Shapes palette and click the arrow (circled here) to open the palette menu. Select All Elements Shapes.

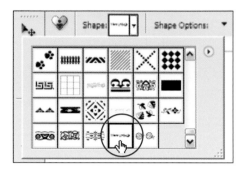

6 Scroll to the bottom of the menu and select the second to last border tile (#5).

TIP *You can view the Custom Shape thumbnails at a larger size by clicking the arrow on the Shapes menu and selecting Large Thumbnail.*

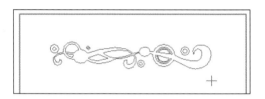

7 Press the Shift key, to keep the shape in proportion, and drag along the top portion of the template starting approximately 3/4-inch from the left edge. Note that a new Shape layer is added to the Layers palette.

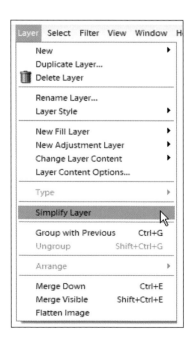

8 Before you can alter the border design in any way, you must first simplify the layer. Choose Layer > Simplify Layer. Select the Zoom tool 🔍, by pressing the Z key on your keyboard. Click to zoom into the border design to approximately 300 percent. The lower left corner of the document window displays the current magnification percentage.

9 Ctrl+click on the Shape 1 layer thumbnail to create an active selection of the border design.

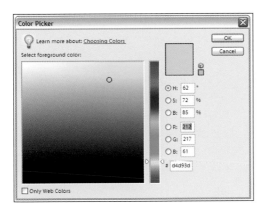

10 Open the Color Picker by clicking on the Foreground Color swatch in the toolbox and select a new color in the Color Field. I selected mustard green (R: 212 G: 217 B: 62). Click OK. Choose Edit > Fill Selection. Make sure Foreground Color is chosen in the Contents Use menu. Click OK. The shape will fill with color.

TIP *To fill an active selection, an object on a layer, or the entire layer quickly with the Foreground color, press Alt+Backspace. To fill an active selection, an object on a layer, or the entire layer quickly with the Background color, press Ctrl+Backspace.*

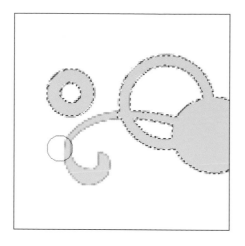

11
Next, the design calls for changing the colors of just the circles in the main part of the border, so it's necessary to deselect all parts of the border except the circles. Select the Selection Brush tool in the toolbox, or press A on your keyboard. Press the Alt key (start with a 10 to 13 pixel-size brush) and brush over the areas that you don't want included in the selection. If you've deselected too much of an area, release the Alt key and brush back over the area.

TIP *Zoom in to 800% to see more detail while you are selecting and deselecting areas of the border. Press the spacebar to temporarily use the Hand tool and drag in the document window to pan different areas. Release the spacebar to continue with the tool you were using.*

TIP *To change the size of your brush quickly, press the left and right bracket keys.*

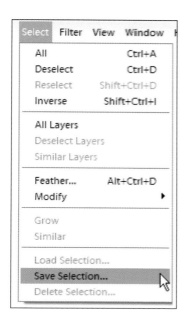

12
After all of that hard work getting an accurate selection, it's a good idea to save it, in case you need to use it again or want to edit it at a later date. If you don't save the selection, you'll have to re-create it all over again. Choose Select > Save Selection and enter a name. For more information on working with Selections, see page 25.

13 To change the color of just the selected circles, open the Color Picker again and select a new color in the Color Field. I chose royal blue (R: 65 G: 44 B: 188). Click OK. Choose Edit > Fill Selection. Make sure Foreground Color is in the Contents Use menu. Click OK. Choose Select > Deselect or Ctrl+D.

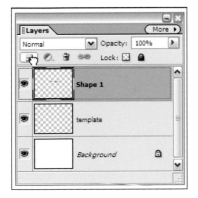

14 Next, duplicate the Shape 1 layer by dragging the layer on top of the New Layer icon, located at the top of the Layers palette.

15 Select the Move tool, press the Shift key to keep the borders aligned, and reposition the duplicated border art at the bottom of the tile.

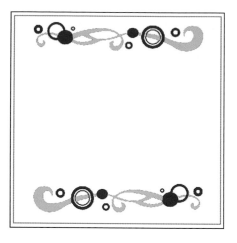

16 Choose Image > Rotate > Flip Layer Horizontal (note: not Flip Horizontal).

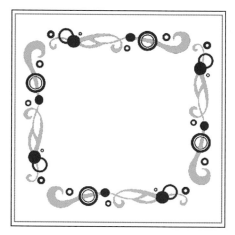

17 Duplicate that Layer, just as you did in step 14, and choose Image > Rotate > Layer 90° Right. Select the Move tool and position the art on the left side of the tile. Now duplicate this layer and choose Image > Rotate > Flip Layer Vertical (note: not Flip Vertical). Position the art on the right side of the tile.

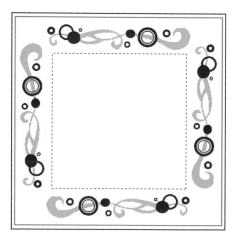

18 Next, create a new layer for the inset rule. Select the Rectangular Marquee tool [⬚]. Make sure the Mode is set back to Normal in the Options bar. Press Shift and drag a selection inside the decorative borders. Use the arrow keys on your keyboard to nudge the selection into place.

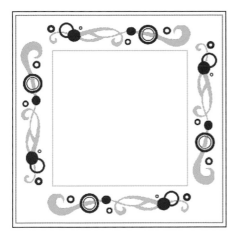

19 Select the Eyedropper tool in the toolbox  and click on an area of green. Green is now your Foreground color. Choose Edit > Stroke (Outline) Selection. Enter a width of 3 pixels and choose Center. Make sure Opacity is set to 100 percent and Preserve Transparency is not checked. Click OK. Choose Select > Deselect or Ctrl+D.

20 Select the Horizontal Type tool T, then click anywhere in the document. Type a number, then highlight the text, and choose your formatting in the Options bar located at the top of your workspace. I selected 212 point Zapf Chancery. Reposition the text with the Move tool. To make the number royal blue, make sure you are on the correct layer, and again use the Eyedropper tool and click on an area of blue. Change the color of the text by pressing Alt+Backspace.

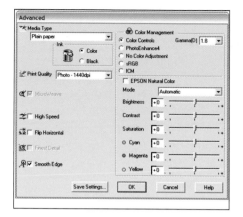

21 Choose File > Save to save the project. Print the artwork onto the smooth, creamy white eggshell side (not the blue tinted side) of the Lazertran inkjet decal paper. Choose File > Page Setup, select Printer in the dialog box and then click on Properties.

Click the Advanced button and then select Plain Paper for Media type, 1440 dpi for Print Quality, and uncheck High Speed. Click OK. These are the settings that work best for an Epson printer according to Lazertran. If you have an HP printer, "Draft" should be a good setting. For more information about printer settings, visit the Lazertran Web site (Lazertran.com) or your printer manufacturer's Web site.

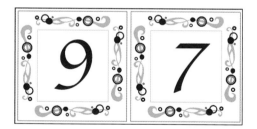

22 Allow the print to dry for at least 30 minutes. With a ruler and craft utility knife, trim the artwork just inside the template lines. Soak the decal in fairly warm water for about 15 seconds (it will curl). Carefully slide the decal off the backing sheet and onto the tile. Gently position it in place. Carefully remove any air bubbles with your fingertips. The decal is extremely delicate, so use a light touch. Allow the decal to dry overnight and then apply several coats of protective varnish, such as oil-based polyurethane.

TIP *Inkjet decal paper and printing inks are expensive! Print your artwork first on plain paper at the most economical setting (fastest) to make sure everything is correct. I do this using the black setting if I'm only evaluating a design and not checking for color.*

CREATING ADDITIONAL MATCHING TILES

To create a copy of all of the tile elements, hide the Background by clicking on the Eye icon in the Layers palette. Create a new layer, and make sure it's positioned above the Background in the Layers palette. Press the Alt key and select Merge Visible from the Layer menu.

Next, link all of the layers, except the newly merged layer and Background. Select the Move tool and press Shift+right arrow key. This will nudge all the elements in 10-pixel increments and keep them aligned to the original number tile.

Select the Text tool, highlight the number, and type in a new one.

POLYMER CLAY ORNAMENTS

These ornaments are really easy to make and will no doubt become cherished keepsakes as the years go by. Imagine your tree if you made one every year! With this project, you will learn how to copy and paste a selection from one document to another, stroke a selection, use the Text tool, and work with inkjet decals and polymer clay.

STUFF YOU WILL NEED

Inkjet decal paper, such as Lazertran, trimmed to 8.5″ x 5.5″

Craft utility knife or cuticle scissors

1/4-inch hole punch

White polymer clay, such as Sculpey Premo!

2-inch diameter wooden dowel, rolling pin, or bottle

Cookie cutters (not to be used with food after use with polymer clay)

Bamboo skewer

Bowl of warm water

Polymer clay glaze, such as Sculpey, gloss or satin finish

Small paint brush

1/4-inch ribbon

1 Open the photo you plan to use for the ornament. Note its resolution by choosing Image > Resize > Image Size. Click OK to close the dialog box.

2 Create a new document by choosing File > New > Blank File. The New dialog box appears. Enter a name in the Name field. Enter 5.5 in the Width field and 8.5 in the Height field. Enter the same resolution as the photo you plan to use. Choose White for Background Contents. Select RGB for Color Mode. Click OK.

3 Select the Elliptical Marquee tool ◯ in the toolbox. Choose Fixed Size from the Mode pop-up menu in the Options bar located at the top of your work area. Enter, in inches, the diameter measurement of the cookie cutter you plan to use in the Height and Width fields.

4 Click on the photo and then position the selection over the area of the image you want on the ornament. Select Edit > Copy or press Ctrl+C on your keyboard. This places a copy of the selected portion of the photo on to your computer clipboard.

Switch back to the blank document, by choosing Window and selecting the name of the document at the bottom of the menu. Choose Edit > Paste, or press Ctrl+V on your keyboard.

5 Note that a copy of your selection is now on its own layer in the Layers palette. Double+click the layer and enter a name.

6 Next, create a new layer, by clicking on the New Layer icon located at the top of the Layers palette. This layer will hold the template for the lower circle of the ornament. Double+click the thumbnail of this layer in the Layers palette and name it "Template".

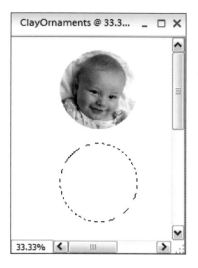

7 Select the Elliptical Marquee tool again (if it isn't still the active tool), and click on the canvas to create a new circular selection.

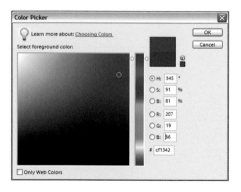

8 Choose the color you want to use for the text, by clicking on the larger Foreground swatch ▣ in the toolbox to open the Color Picker. Either select a color in the Color Field, or float your cursor over different areas of your photo. Your cursor will change into the Eyedropper ✐, enabling you to sample a specific color in your image. Click on the desired color and then click OK.

9 Before you add the text, stroke the selection, which will later be used as a template, so you can accurately cut out the second circle. Choose Edit > Stroke (Outline) Selection. Enter 2 pixels and click OK. Deselect the selection by choosing Ctrl+D.

10 Next, choose the Horizontal Text tool **T** in the toolbox by pressing T on your keyboard, and click on your document. Type what you would like and then click and drag over the text to highlight it. Choose your formatting in the Options bar located at the top of your work area. I chose the font Leftovers. Position the text with the Move tool or by nudging it, using the arrow keys on your keyboard. Click outside the text in the document window. Press Ctrl+S to save the file.

TIP *The Leftovers font is available free at www.fontdiner.com.*

11 When you are ready to print onto the inkjet decal paper, follow the directions provided by the transfer paper manufacturer. Allow the print to dry for at least 30 minutes. Trim the photo, and then trim the other circle just inside the template lines. You may find cuticle scissors easier to use for this task than a craft utility knife. Punch a hole at the top and the bottom of each decal circle.

Warm up a piece of clay in your hands, until it is soft and pliable. Roll it out onto a smooth surface (one that's not used for food), to a thickness of approximately 1/4". Use the cookie cutter to cut out the shapes.

12 Soak the decal in fairly warm water for about 15 seconds (it will curl). Carefully slide the decal off of the backing sheet and onto the clay. Gently position it in place. Carefully remove any air bubbles with your finger tips. The decal is extremely delicate, so use a light touch.

Place the clay pieces on a foil-lined baking sheet, and bake the clay in a preheated 275° oven for approximately 5-7 minutes. Keep a watchful eye, because they can turn brown quickly. Allow the clay to cool thoroughly. Apply a few coats of polymer clay glaze with a small, fine paint brush. Allow the glaze to dry. When the oven cools, wipe down the inside with baking soda and water.

13 Cut two pieces of ribbon, one 14-inch long, the other 8-inch long. Tie a slip knot at the top of the longest piece of ribbon. Thread it through the top hole on the top piece of clay from front to back and then through the bottom hole from back to front. Loop it over the bottom edge of the clay, and back through the bottom hole to secure it.

Repeat threading the ribbon through the bottom piece of clay. Next, thread the shorter piece of ribbon through the bottom hole and tie a knot with all three pieces approximately one-quarter inch below the clay. Trim the tail so each ribbon has the same length.

HOLIDAY GIFT WRAP

Once you learn how easy it is to create your own gift wrap, you'll be hooked. Here,

the focus is a holiday theme, but you'll soon understand how to create a pattern for any

occasion. With this project, you will learn how to use the custom Shape tool, transform

shapes, apply colors using the Swatches palette, and create your own custom photo brush.

11 x 17 glossy or semi-glossy photo stock

1 Create a new file by choosing File > New > Blank File. In the Name field enter "HollyGiftWrap". Enter 11 inches in the Width field and 17 inches in the Height field.

Enter the resolution of your chosen photo. To learn its resolution, choose File > Open to open the photo, and then choose Image > Resize > Image Size. Check the resolution, then click Cancel to close the dialog box.

Choose White for Background Contents. Select RGB for Color Mode. Click OK.

2 Open the Color Swatches palette by choosing Window > Color Swatches. Choose Window from the pop-up menu for a wider range of colors and then select a holly green.

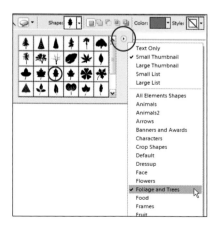

3 Next, select the Custom Shape tool 💬 in the toolbox (by pressing U a few times on your keyboard to toggle through the Shapes tools). From the Options bar, located at the top of your work area, open the Shapes palette and click the arrow (circled here) to open the palette menu. Select Foliage and Trees and then the holly leaf (Leaf 6).

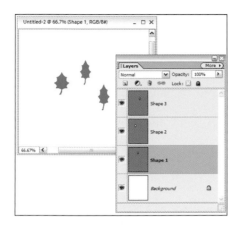

4 Drag anywhere on your canvas to create the first leaf, approximately 1/4-inch in size. (Pressing Shift while you drag will keep the leaf in proportion.) Notice a Shape layer is created in the Layers palette. Release the Shift key and then draw another leaf. By releasing the Shift key after drawing, each leaf will then be on its own layer. Add another leaf.

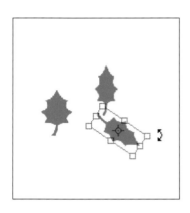

5 Select the Move tool ▶⊕ and click on one of the leaves. A bounding box appears around the shape. To resize a leaf, drag a cornerpoint. To rotate a leaf, hold your cursor a short distance away from a cornerpoint. When the curved arrows appear as your cursor, click and drag to rotate in the desired direction. Press Enter to apply the transformation. Press Escape (Esc) to cancel the transformation. Repeat this step for the other two leaves. Use the arrow keys on your keyboard to reposition the leaves.

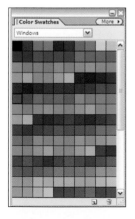

6 Next, choose red in the Swatches palette. Then select the Ellipse Shape tool ⬭ in the toolbox. Once again, to toggle through the Shape tools in the toolbox, press U.

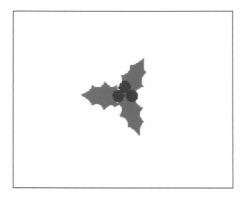

7 Press Shift and drag to draw a small berry. Press the Ctrl key to temporarily activate the Move tool, and place the berry on top of the leaves. Create two more berries and position them on top of the leaves. In the Layers palette, drag the berry layer to the top, so that the berries overlay everything else.

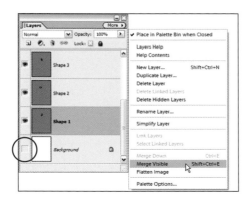

8 The next step is to merge the Shape layers. This will make it easy to duplicate the holly art for the pattern. Click the Eye icon of the Background in the Layers palette to hide it. Make sure one of the Shape layers is active and then choose Merge Visible from the Layers palette menu. All of the shapes are now on one layer. If you wish, click the Eye icon to make the Background visible once again.

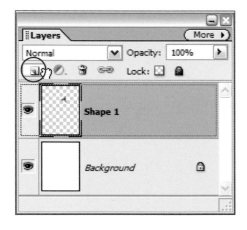

9 Next, duplicate this merged layer, by dragging it on top of the New Layer icon located at the top of the Layers palette. An exact duplicate of your holly cluster is now laying directly on top of your original.

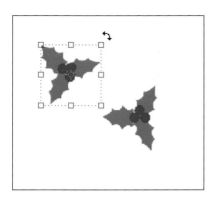

10 Select the Move tool in the toolbox and click and drag on the duplicate to reposition it. Rotate the duplicated artwork as you did in step 5. While the art is selected, you can also nudge it around with the arrow keys. Press Enter to apply the repositioning, once you are satisfied.

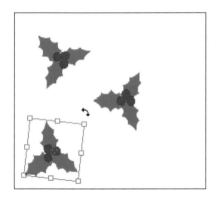

11 Repeat steps 9 and 10, to have three separate clusters of holly leaves and berries. If you plan to add photo circles to your design, be mindful of leaving space in your pattern.

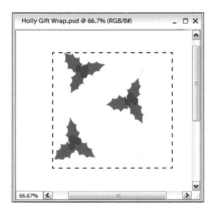

Holly Gift Wrap.psd @ 66.7% (RGB/8#)

66.67%

12 Select the Rectangular Marquee tool ⬚ and make sure Normal is selected for the Mode in the Options bar located at the top of your work area. Press the Shift key and drag a square around all three holly clusters. Keep in mind that you will want to include a bit of extra space in your selection, to accommodate the photo brush design you create in the following steps. Choose Define Pattern from Selection from the Edit menu.

13 Enter a name for your pattern in the Custom Pattern dialog box and click OK. Make sure you deselect your selection by pressing Ctrl+D.

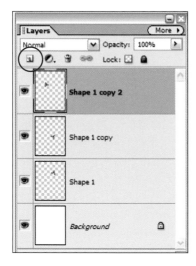

14 Create a new layer by clicking on the New Layer icon located at the top of the Layers palette. Drag the layer to the top of the layer stack.

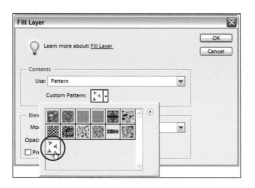

15 Choose Edit > Fill Layer and then choose Pattern from the Contents > Use pop-up list. Click on the Custom Pattern menu, locate your pattern, and then click OK. The layer fills with the pattern.

16 Choose Save from the File menu. You could stop now, if you wish, and print your gift wrap, or continue and add the photo circles. The art shown here is a second pattern I created to better accommodate the photo circles.

17 Next, open the photo that you want to use as the custom brush, by choosing File > Open.

18 Select the Elliptical Marquee Tool ◯ in the toolbox, by pressing just the letter "M" on your keyboard. Make sure the Mode is set to Normal in the Options bar located at the top of your work area. Press the Shift key, and drag a circle around the area that you want to define as your custom brush.

19 Choose Edit > Define Brush from Selection and enter a name. Note that the selected area of the image is displayed in black and white. This is because custom brushes can only be used with one color. The number below the image indicates the pixel diameter of the brush. Click OK.

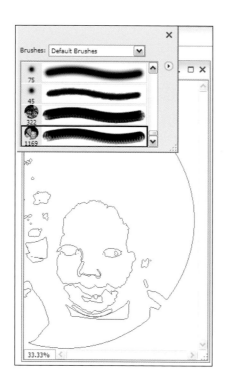

20 Select the Brush Tool ✐ in the toolbox, and then click on the triangle in the Brush style menu in the Options bar, located at the top of your work area. Choose Default Brushes. Scroll down to the bottom of the list and select your new custom brush. Note that your cursor is now in the shape of your custom brush.

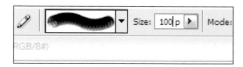

21 Change the size of the brush in the Options bar, located at the top of your work area. Choose an appropriate size for your brush (your cursor will display an outline of it when you float it over your canvas).

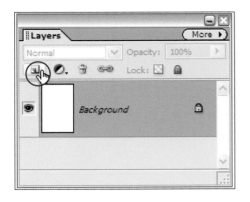

22 Now it's time for some experi-mentation. Create a new blank layer by clicking on the New Layer icon 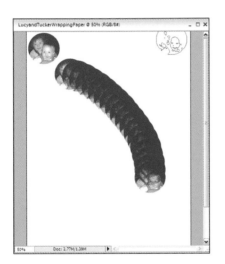 located at the top of the Layers palette.

A new blank layer gives you the flexibil-ity to experiment because you can later discard it.

23 Click once, anywhere on your page to see the results of the custom brush. Next, click and drag across the page. Notice the brush design is overlapping. Select Edit > Undo or press Control+Z to undo the previous action.

24 To adjust the spacing, click on the brush next to the right of "More Options" in the Options bar. Enter 150 in the Spacing field, then click and drag across the page. Experiment with other settings until you achieve the spacing you need for your design.

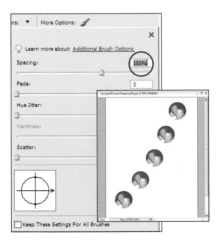

25 When you have finished experimenting, discard the layer by dragging it to the Trash icon located at the top of the Layers palette. Create a new layer by clicking the New Layer icon .

26 Click anywhere you would like on your canvas with your custom brush, or click and drag to apply the spaced pattern you built in step 24 and 25. Press the Shift key to draw a straight horizontal or vertical line. If you want to use two colors as I have, create a new layer, select a new color in the Swatches palette, and continue with your design.

Save the File by choosing File > Save. Print your design on glossy photo stock and allow it to dry completely before wrapping your gift.

TUMBLED MARBLE COASTERS

The image I designed for this project appears much more complicated than it actually is. By adding self-adhesive felt to the back of the tiles, you'll have a unique set of coasters. If you want to use the Gerbera daisy image, you can download it from www.photoshopcrafts. com. With this project, you will learn how to silhouette an image using the Magic Selection Brush tool, create a custom gradient, experiment with Blending Modes, and apply filters such as Clouds and Noise.

Four 4-inch tumbled marble tiles

Inkjet decal paper, such as Lazertran

Craft utility knife

Turpentine

Bowl of warm water

Oil-based varnish, such as polyurethane

Small paint brush

Two 9 x 12 sheets adhesive-backed felt, such as Quick Stick

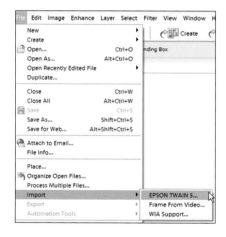

1 The main graphic for the coasters is a silk Gerbera daisy which I put directly onto the bed of a scanner. To access a scanner that is hooked up to your computer, choose File > Import and select the name of your scanner manufacturer. The scanner software dialog box opens, and it is there where you select the resolution and the area of the image you want to scan. The image then opens in Photoshop Elements.

2 The next step is to select just the flower. In this case, it will be much faster to select the background because of the similarity in tonal colors. Select the Magic Selection Brush tool in the toolbox and click once on the background. Notice now that your cursor has a + sign next to it. This means that you can continue adding to your selection by clicking in areas not yet selected.

NOTE *Elements Version 3.0 users can select the background area of the image with the Magic Wand tool.*

3 If you pick up some of the flower pixels, switch to the Magic Selection Brush tool that has a - next to the cursor in the Options bar located at the top of your work area. Click on the area that you don't want to be part of the selection.

4 Next, since you ultimately want the subject selected (not the background), you need to select the inverse of the selected area by choosing Select > Inverse. Now the flower is selected.

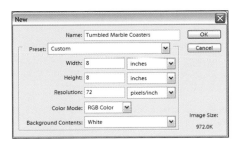

5 Create a new document by choosing File > New > Blank File. The New dialog box appears. Enter a name in the Name field. Enter 8 inches in the Width field and 8 inches in the Height field. Enter the same resolution as your scanned image. If you're using the image of the daisy from the www.photoshopcrafts.com Web site, enter 72 for resolution. Choose White for Background Contents. Select RGB for Color Mode. Click OK.

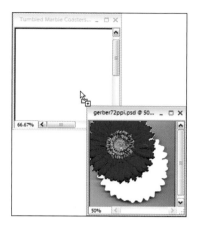

6 Select the Move tool ▶⊕ in the toolbox, and with the Shift key pressed, drag and drop the selection into the blank document. When you press the Shift key while dragging an image from one document to another, the image is automatically centered in the new document. Note that the flower is now on its own layer in the Layers palette.

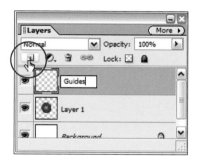

7 Create a new layer by clicking on the New Layer icon located at the top of the Layers palette. Double+click the layer and name it "Guides". Press D on your keyboard to set the Foreground and Background swatches in the toolbox back to the default black and white.

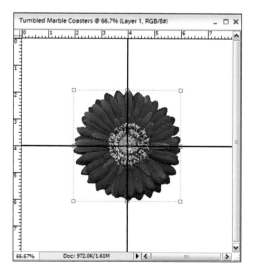

8 Choose Rulers from the View menu. Select the Pencil tool in the toolbox by pressing N on your keyboard. In the Options bar located at the top of your work area, enter 2 pixels for Size.

Now, press the Shift key and drag a vertical line from the top of your document to the bottom, at the 4-inch mark on the ruler. Release the mouse button. Now, drag a horizontal line also at the 4-inch mark, with the Shift key pressed.

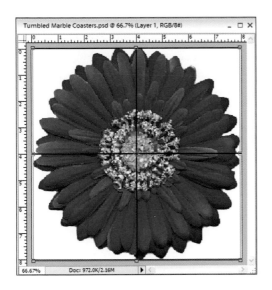

9 The next step is to scale the flower to the size of the entire canvas. Select the Move tool in the toolbox by pressing V on your keyboard, and then click on the flower layer. Press Shift and drag the corner points. Remember to use the arrow keys on your keyboard to nudge the flower into place. The side, top, and bottom handles should line up with the guides. Press Enter to apply the transformation. Once positioned, you can discard the Guides layer by dragging it on top of the Trash icon located at the top of the Layers palette.

10 To add a gradient to the Background, select the Gradient tool ▭ in the toolbox by pressing G on your keyboard. Click the Radial Gradient icon in the Options bar located at the top of your work area, and then click the Edit button to open the Gradient Editor dialog box.

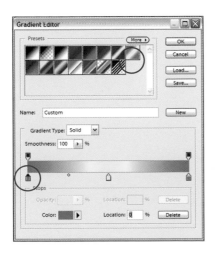

11 Select the "Orange Yellow Orange" gradient, as shown here, and then click once on the left Color Stop located in the lower left area of the dialog box. This will enable you to change the color of the first section of the gradient in the following step. You know it's selected when the triangle is black.

12 Float your cursor over the image. Your cursor will change into an eyedropper 🖋, enabling you to sample a specific color in your image. Click on the desired color. You can also double+click the Color Stop to open the Color Picker and choose a color there.

13 Designate the length of a color and where it transitions into the next color by dragging the small diamond to the left or right, as shown here. To avoid saving over one of the default gradients, enter a name for the gradient and click the New button. Click OK. Your custom gradient is now saved within the Gradient Editor and can be used another time.

14 With the Background selected in the Layers palette, drag across the image with the Gradient tool. Experiment dragging in different directions and lengths.

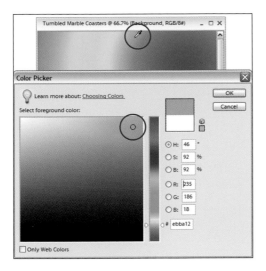

15 A different technique you can use on the background, instead of the gradient, is to apply the Clouds filter which randomly mixes two colors in a "cloud-like" fashion.

Click on the Foreground swatch in the toolbox to open the Color Picker. Float your cursor over the image. Your cursor will change into an eyedropper, enabling you to sample a specific color in your image. Click on the desired color and then click OK.

Next, click on the Background swatch in the toolbox and sample a second color. Click OK. When you apply the Clouds filter in the next step, the new Foreground and Background colors you just selected will be mixed.

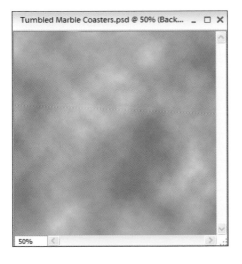

16 Select the Background in the Layers palette. Select Filter > Render > Clouds. Experiment toggling through different cloud combinations, by pressing Ctrl+F a few times.

17 Next, change the Blending Mode for the flower layer by first selecting that layer in the Layers palette. Choose Overlay from the Blending Mode pop-up menu in the Layers palette. The Overlay mode combines the pixels of the active layer with the underlying image pixels, but preserves the highlight and shadow detail in the image.

18 Press the Alt key and then choose Merge Visible from the Layers palette menu. This will make a merged copy of the two layers onto a new layer, so the mezzotint effect can be applied to both the Background clouds and the flower. To create a mezzotint effect, add Noise to the image by choosing Filter > Noise > Add Noise.

19 The final design step is to add a few lines of text to the image. I used the Latin terms for genus and species of the Gerbera daisy, along with a few other historical word associations relevant to this flower.

Select the Horizontal Text tool **T** in the toolbox and click anywhere in your document. Type what you would like.

20 Drag over the text to highlight it, and choose your formatting in the Options bar located at the top of your work area. I selected Snell Roundhand at various point sizes for each line of text. Select the Move tool in the toolbox to position each line of text.

21 When you are ready to print onto the inkjet decal paper, follow the directions provided by the transfer paper manufacturer. Allow the print to dry for at least 30 minutes. With a ruler and craft utility knife, trim the image so each quadrant is exactly 4-inches wide.

22 Brush the tiles with a coat of turpentine (do not substitute mineral spirits). This will help the transfer settle into the pores of the marble.

Soak the decal in fairly warm water for about 15 seconds (it will curl). Carefully slide the decal off the backing sheet and onto the marble. Gently position it in place and carefully remove any air bubbles with your fingertips. The decal is extremely delicate, so use a light touch. Allow the decal to dry overnight, and then apply several coats of oil-based protective varnish, such as polyurethane.

The final step is to trim the felt backing sheets just under 4-square inches for each coaster. I applied two squares of self-adhesive felt to the back of each coaster for added surface protection.

GIFT BOX TEMPLATE

Enlarge this template on a copy machine 134%. Make two copies and use one for practice.

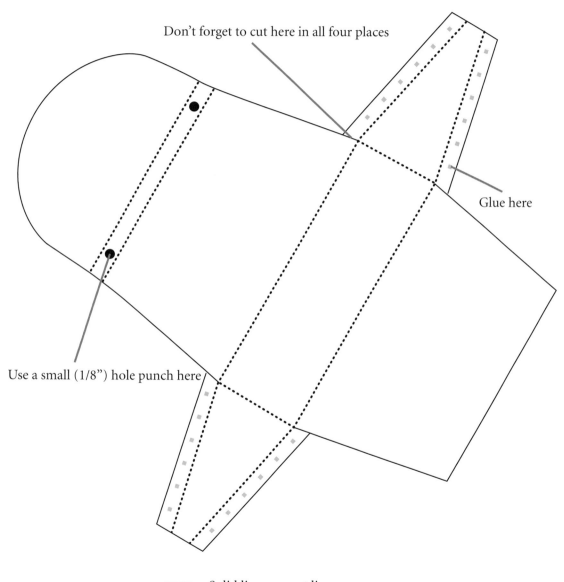

Don't forget to cut here in all four places

Glue here

Use a small (1/8") hole punch here

—— Solid lines are cut lines

••••• Dotted lines are score and fold lines

▪ ▪ Dashes are for glue

CREDITS

Photography, painting, and craft credits:

Doug Carson	*"Axel"*	*page 11*
Sonya Carson	*"Finger Painting"*	*pages 26-27*
Scott Cowlin	*"Daphne"*	*pages 35-41*
Stanley and Mary K. Fitzgerald	*"Wedding"*	*pages 49-51*
Jane Greis	*"Jamison and Cameron"*	*pages 61-65, 123-128*
Susan Krantz	*"Needlepoint and sewing"*	*pages 87, 91*
Eva-Gitta Nabih	*"Potato Hands"*	*pages 53, 55-59*
	"Sonya"	*page 11*
	"Lucy"	*page 11*
Karen Reichstein	*"Pug"*	*page 8*
	"Dutch Gnomes"	*pages 9,11*
	"Puerto Rico Beach"	*pages 100-109*
	"Carole"	*pages 99, 106-109*
Julie Vician	*"Lucy and Tucker"*	*pages 135-138*
Jeff Weldon	*"Buddy"*	*pages 88-90*

All other photography and artwork by Elizabeth Bulger and Stephen Sakowich.

INDEX